Joy
In Suffering

Rosemary Pope

Joy
In Suffering

A *memoir* of one couple's pregnancy losses
and how they found happiness

ROSEMARY POPE

Carpenter's Son Publishing

Joy in Suffering

©2019 by Rosemary Pope

Published by Carpenter's Son Publishing, Franklin, Tennessee

Published in association with Larry Carpenter of Christian Book Services, LLC
www.christianbookservices.com

Scripture taken from THE STUDENT BIBLE, NEW INTERNATIONAL VERSION®, NIV® Copyright © 1973, 1978, 1984, 2011 by Biblica, Inc.™ Used by permission. All rights reserved worldwide.

Cover Photo by Paul Sokal. www.imaginography.net

Newborn Photos by Sarah Ward. www.sarahsviewphoto.com

Edited by Robert Irvin

Cover and Interior Design by Suzanne Lawing

Printed in the United States of America

978-1-946889-84-3

Dedication

To my children.
May you never wonder how much
your Dad and I love you all.

Acknowledgements

To my Lord and Savior: I cannot fathom a life without You. For better or worse, You have always been there. There are not enough words to describe my gratitude and thankfulness for Your presence in my life.

To Dad, Mom, Pops, Michele: you have always been ears to listen, voices of wisdom, and arms to hold us when there was nothing to say. Thank you for raising, guiding, and loving us.

To every midwife I've personally known and worked with: you have all been like angels in disguise. My life has been better knowing every single one of you. Your knowledge and attention to detail is invaluable. Thank you all for the wisdom and discernment used in caring for my children and me.

To every doctor and nurse who has stepped in to provide the extra level of care that my babies and I have needed: all of you have been there in ways no one else could. I am forever thankful and grateful for your expertise in my times of need.

To all our family and friends who walked with me through this time in my life: you all hold a special place in my heart. I will never forget the sincerity of your relationships and how emotionally involved you all were. The love and support Bobby and I have had is one of the greatest blessings anyone could have this side of Heaven. Thank you all from the bottom of my heart.

To Bobby, aka Trey, you've stepped up to the plate time and time again to hold the promise of our vows—for better or worse, in sickness and in health. Not that I ever expected different when I married you, but I find myself highly blessed to be married to such a man as yourself. Thank you for continuing to give of yourself day in and day out, no matter the season of life. I love you.

Foreword

If you're extremely blessed, you sometimes get to meet someone who makes you a better person just because you've had the opportunity to know them. I have been blessed to know Rosemary and Bobby Pope almost since the beginning of the journey you are about to read. I have watched them walk through both the joys and sorrows and been privileged to have a ringside seat to much of their story. I was amazed at the depth of their faith in the beginning of their story, and I watched it grow deeper and more certain as their journey to parenthood continued.

Not many walk the journey they have had the honor of walking. Almost all would say that is a good thing. It's certainly not what a young girl dreams of as she considers the journey to motherhood that will someday be hers. However, I have found that the Lord works through the times of greatest difficulties in our lives to mold us more into His image, to build us up to have all we need to fulfill the plans He has for us. Rosemary Pope is indeed a woman in whom the likeness of Christ is readily seen, and as you will read, He carried her faithfully every step of the way.

Rosemary shares, with great honesty, the times of strong faith as well as the times of hurt and questioning. But at the heart of it all, there is a deep, abiding faith that has kept her relationship with Jesus strong and growing no matter what. She knows Jeremiah 29:11 to be true in the most difficult days a mother can walk through, and in the times of greatest joy a mother can feel.

I know your faith will be strengthened as you read this story of one family's loss and heartache and the redemption that only a God who loves us immeasurably can bring. As you read her story, you have the opportunity to connect with the same Jesus who ministered to Rosemary on her journey. He's there for you, too, and He loves you just as deeply. He longs to walk your road with you—no matter where you may find yourself today.

May you be blessed with the peace of God as you keep your eyes fixed on Him!

Kelly Miller

One

When I was a senior in high school the PTA made these spiral-bound keepsake books for my graduating class. In each one was a little something about the student. Things like, "Where do you see yourself in ten years?" I remember my answer vividly: "To be married to my high school sweetheart, a youth pastor's wife, and a mom."

I didn't know what I wanted as a career, but I was sure those three things were bound to happen.

My husband, Bobby, and I started dating when I was a freshman and he was a sophomore. I had just turned fourteen and he was about to be sixteen. We shared the same Spanish class together, a class mixed with different grade levels. The teacher placed us in alphabetical order by our last names. Mine being Rains and his Pope, he wound up sitting directly in front of me.

As I think back to my first day of high school, I remember feeling nervous. I was so intimidated by everyone older than me, just as nearly all new students are.

Spanish was my third class of the day. Starting to get the hang of things, I arrived and was seated before the bell rang. I was excited and relieved to see familiar faces. We chatted for a few moments until the bell sounded for class to start.

As the bell rings, in walks Bobby Pope with a big smile on his face; he was clearly making his presence known. I tried to hide my immediate interest in him, but inside I felt butterflies and my face began to blush.

He had semi-short, wavy, blond hair, parted down the middle. He also had light greenish-gray eyes and a carefree grin to match his playful spirit. And this: he had been voted "most friendliest" the year before.

Oh, but that boy scared me. He may have been easy on the eyes, but he had also been labeled a troublemaker. His freshman year was full of rebellion. Sneaking off to parties, drinking—your typical teenage boy. Everything I was against.

I did not want those things for myself. I simply had no desire. I knew I had to keep cool and remain distant from him. Besides, what would someone like him want with a sweet, innocent freshman?

We were a few weeks into school and a couple of boys had shown interest in me. This was something new for me, because any guy I had been close to before had simply been a friend. For one reason or another those boys came and went. During that time, I set aside my fondness of Bobby and told myself I would focus on just being friends.

That is all I ever saw us as because he was one of the cool ones and I was a mediocre ninth-grader. There was no need to let my mind wonder about anything more. I did find Bobby to be a little peculiar after things broke off between the last boy and myself. The day it happened, Bobby wanted to know all the minute details of how it all went down—when, where, why, and how.

There wasn't much to tell him because it all happened so fast. The kid and I just weren't into each other, so it was nothing devastating. I do remember that boy sent his friend to tell me we were over. He was extremely shy, and it all just seemed sort of laughable.

I told Bobby everything. I was surprised he wanted to know, but I also didn't think too deeply about the why.

A couple of weeks went by and I found myself letting my guard down. We would talk in class with everyone, but something more started to happen. Our Spanish class was at one end of the school. We both had math at the other end, and right next door to each other. Bobby would wait on me to gather my things and walk next to me, continuing our conversation until we reached our destination. This simple act of him walking with me in front of our peers every day put me in touch with my feelings toward him. I allowed myself to think that maybe, just maybe, he might care a little about me too.

It was the beginning of October when we received our school pictures. Bobby asked if he could have a print of mine. Blushing, I answered "no." My reasoning was that this was my mom's order, and she was going to send copies to my relatives.

That answer sufficed for the moment, but the next day he came to school with a small photo album; it contained only about two or three pictures. One was a wallet-size school picture of himself. Sliding it out of the plastic cover, he handed it to me. He asked if I had gotten my mom's permission to give him one of mine. I hadn't even asked her because I hadn't taken him seriously. I had been pretty certain he didn't really mean it when he asked for one.

Toward the end of class that day, Bobby turned to me and asked, "Who do you like?" I am pretty certain all the color drained from my face and I turned quite pale. Why had he asked me?

I pondered a moment, then responded, "I'm the kind of person who doesn't like to say who she has a crush on." *Lame*, I thought to myself. The answer was not a good one, and it led to him playing the guessing game, naming off different boys.

The bell rang for class to dismiss and it was time for our usual stroll across campus. As we walked, the thought that he may actually have feelings toward me entered my mind. My stomach in knots, I decided to try *him* at this guessing game.

"I know who you like," I said.

"You do?" he questioned. "Who is it?"

I paused a moment to think, and then, with a wry smile, answered, "You like me."

With a look of confusion, Bobby replied, "How did you know?"

I scurried to find an answer. "Oh, it was obvious with you wanting my picture and all." I could feel my heart drumming, but I now felt it was safe to let him in on my feelings. "I actually like you too."

I do not recall much else of our conversation. I'm sure we walked the rest of the way kind of speechless.

It didn't take long before we were immersed in each other's lives. Getting to know each other came quite easily for us. We never seemed to run out of things to talk about. We were best friends and each other's confidant.

Our town was a small one. Everyone knew everyone, and if they didn't, they knew someone who did. Bobby had—and still does have—a confident personality. When you mix that with the impressions people around town had of him, it led to my parents being less than thrilled that I was interested in this boy.

I am their firstborn, oldest of three girls, and here came this boy they felt could ruin me and my innocence. Their precious baby girl . . . my poor parents.

Despite his confidence, Bobby never could find the right words to say to my parents. He is the oldest of three rowdy boys. Whenever they were in a room together . . . well, it was a test to my nerves and my growing love for him.

I knew deep down that however my parents saw him, Bobby truly was one of the good ones. Others might have seen us as a strong couple, but we had our issues. His parents were youth pastors and did their best to keep us accountable, but they couldn't be there to watch our every move. We were like most teenage boys and girls: given the opportunity, we'd get carried away and take things a little too far; this happened a couple of times. But we always stopped just shy of the act intended for marriage. Sure, Bobby tried a couple of times, but as soon as he could tell I wasn't having it, he would stop. Every time. In this way, he showed great respect for me.

During Bobby's senior year, he had a teacher who prided himself on dispensing wisdom about life and English. This man was one of the most respected teachers in the school and an instant favorite of anyone in his classroom. One day, the teacher decided to speak to the girls. He told them that if they *didn't* have sex with their boyfriends, they would end up marrying the boy. Bobby spoke up and told him he was wrong. He said he was about to break up with his girlfriend (me) because she wouldn't have sex with him. We had been dating about two and a half years at this point.

After class, Bobby was eager to find me; he was certain he would prove his teacher wrong by giving me an ultimatum. He told me the story, and all I could do was laugh. I told him his teacher was absolutely right. I was not going to compromise my standards, I said, and that was why he was going to marry me. He was openmouthed at my response, but he knew I was right. He actually began to laugh with me at how ridiculous he'd been. In that moment I knew, without any doubt, we were going to marry someday.

The day before my senior year of high school was the day Bobby left for college. His family and I drove Bobby and his belongings to Abilene Christian University (ACU), about three hours away, to attend college and run track. Actually, his parents drove his belongings and I rode with Bobby in the new truck he had received as a graduation gift, a white 2003 GMC Sierra with a cab and a half and a side step. Even though he was moving, I knew we would be just fine. Riding with him in that truck felt like home to me. I knew this moment of separation in our lives would not last long and that we'd be together again soon. We laughed and laughed during that ride; we still roar with laughter at some of the inside jokes we created that day.

But it also ended up being a sad goodbye. Mainly for his

mama, but it was heart-tugging to me too. But deep inside, I knew the separation wasn't for long, so I stayed positive. On the drive back, though, I began to mope a bit—the reality was starting to set in. I called him when I got home, called him the next morning, and again that night! It was different without him at school, but it was positive in other ways. I got to experience high school without a care about boys, and I just enjoyed my last year of high school with my friends. It was actually quite freeing. Besides, Bobby's brother Josh had football games every Friday, so Bobby used the excuse of not wanting to miss any of his games to drive home on weekends.

While Bobby was home for the Christmas holidays, he took me to a jewelry store to look at wedding rings. I did not think much of this visit. I knew we would get married eventually, but I was still a senior in high school; to me, this was really just a date for fun. It was a chance to dream about our future. I had the thought of being OK with a plain solitaire diamond, but I soon realized the tags on those rings were not-so-in-our-price-range. I eventually landed on a sweet simple set of bands with a marquise cut diamond in the middle. It made me smile seeing it on my hand, but I didn't let my heart land on that exact set. What were the chances, I thought, of getting that same pair of rings later on down the road?

Toward the end of January, Bobby met with my dad and asked his blessing to marry me. Despite what he may have thought about him, Dad gave his support.

My youngest sister, Mackenzie, was turning six and we went to dinner with my family at the Rainforest Café. My mom made sure I brought my fancy camera for the occasion.

Everything went along as normal; we visited and ate dinner. After the main course, my dad asked for my camera. Not thinking anything of it, I handed it to him. I figured we were about to sing Happy Birthday, eat cake, and open presents.

As he got the camera ready, I asked, "Dad, will you take a picture of Bobby and me?"

His response? "Sure. Like a before and after." I leaned into Bobby and smiled. *Click.*

I'm sure I had a look of confusion, wondering what my dad meant by this, when Bobby stood up and pulled his chair out of the way. I turned to see what he was doing and found him going down on one knee. He pulled out a small velvety black box, cracked it open, and showed me the identical set of rings I had picked out the month before.

He asked the modest but extremely weighted question: "Will you marry me?"

I think I mostly felt awe. I looked up, smiled, and said, "Yes."

I was certain I had answered correctly. We hugged, kissed, and Bobby slid the rings on my finger. The perfect size. I turned toward my family, who was all smiles.

My dad, still holding the camera, said, "Now, how about that 'after'?" We gladly posed for more photos.

Most of my classmates who knew us well were happy for us. Bobby's brother Josh did the school announcements over the intercom every day. He showed his support by congratulating us for the entire school to hear. If people weren't excited for us, they didn't voice it. One girl said she could never imagine being engaged in high school. I didn't take it as an insult; she was trying to picture herself in this position and simply could not see it.

I showed the rings to a few of my closest teachers. They all gave cautionary smiles. I knew it was hard for them to express full approval. Only a few voiced their concerns, but I did not let this get me down. I knew they meant their cautionary approaches out of love.

The rest of that spring semester flew by. Not long after the proposal I went on a trip to Disney World, danced in my school's annual spring show (the dancing was with our school's drill team, which I was part of). I also went skiing over spring break with my grandparents, to prom with a couple of girlfriends, won grand champion for a painting at the county fair, took another artwork to the state competition . . . and eventually graduated. Sure I was engaged, but I didn't think much past living in those last high school moments. I wanted to soak it all in.

Once graduation was over, Bobby and I began to talk about our commitment to one another. We realized we didn't want to spend any more time apart than necessary and wanted to begin the rest of our lives together—sooner rather than later. We talked with our parents, made a plan, and set a date: August 19, 2006. Exactly one month after my eighteenth birthday.

We pulled our wedding together in six weeks and had close to three hundred guests in attendance. Managing to pull everything together with little time and a modest budget, our ceremony was held in the midst of . . . cow patties and meadow muffins in my family's pasture. The reception was held in the backyard of Bobby's parents' home. We had sandwiches for dinner and a dance floor made of plywood and two-by-fours with baby powder spread across it for easy sliding!

We had our first dance to a George Strait classic, "I Cross My Heart." The lyrics to that song warmed my heart, but I couldn't grasp the true emphasis of their meaning and just how relevant they'd come to be. They speak of the nature of unconditional love and . . . the storms that are sure to come.

We celebrated a while longer. But Bobby was quite eager to do what he'd been looking forward to the past four years. He did not want to wait any longer; he wanted his prize. Honestly, I was nervous and scared. He surprised me with a two-night stay at the Gaylord Texan. Wanting to make this night extra special, he had arrived at the hotel earlier that day to set up candles and spread rose petals around the room. Once we arrived, he did not rush me. We took our time, making it sweet, special, something to be remembered.

Finally, husband and wife.

"But at the beginning of creation God 'made them male and female.' For this reason a man will leave his father and mother and be united to his wife, and the two will become one flesh. So they are no longer two, but one. (Mark 10:6-8, NIV).

Two

After our wedding, we settled in a little townhome close to ACU in Abilene. I enrolled in a satellite campus of Cisco Junior College down the road and was a cashier at a local Albertson's grocery store. It was a simple time for us, getting our feet wet in the married life; there was not much to stress about. For fun, we would Rollerblade and skate around campus, play ultimate frisbee with his college buddies, dove hunt in a local farmer's field, watch VHS movies from the video store, or stay up beyond reasonable limits to play a card game of Pounce with our friends. Occasionally, we'd drive a little farther west to some land that had been passed down through generations in my mother's family. It used to be a dairy farm, but in more recent years it had become a place to go camping and hunting.

After the end of the school year in May, we decided to move back home into a quaint one-bedroom apartment. College was fun, but we could tell it wasn't for us at this time in our lives. Despite the recession, Bobby began working for the family business of building homes. I got a job at the day care my youngest sister attended. Life seemed to move quickly, but we had no real aim. We had a lot of figuring out, a lot of growing up to do. After all, we were only 19 and 20.

While working at the day care, I met a family I would babysit for from time to time. They had two girls and were expecting a third. We seemed to click quite well. The girls were absolutely precious. One evening the mom asked if I would come nanny for their family. I wasn't happy working at the day care, and I adored this family. It didn't take much convincing of myself to take this job. I wanted to say yes as soon as she asked me, but I didn't want to appear desperate. Not long after, I put in my notice at the day care so I could begin working for them.

My job as nanny consisted of cooking the girls meals, teaching them basic preschool knowledge, playing, reading, putting them down for naps, and doing their laundry. I loved every bit of the work. It was hard not to mention this family to those I came across outside of work because they became like a second family to me. They were very giving; it never felt like work to me. We'd go to the Dallas Zoo, Arboretum, mall, local library, and the park. I'd also take the girls to their swim class and dance lessons.

And I was also able to watch, firsthand, what it was like to bring a new baby into the home. Since I was the oldest in my family, I had experienced this before, but not from the perspective of a grown-up. Seeing the nursery painted lavender, the new bedding and décor straight from Land of Nod and Pottery Barn . . . it was all sweet perfection. Boxes of hand-me-down clothes, car seats, strollers, playpens, bottles, and more were brought down from the attic, and mounds of diapers were brought home from work showers. I was able to hear the heartbeat and decorate "big sister" shirts for the big day.

I remember the day this precious baby girl was born. She was to arrive via Cesarean section (because mom had to have an emergency C-section with her sisters) and her birthday was strategically planned for a Friday in September 2008. I arrived early that morning to the bustle of her parents getting ready for the hospital instead of work. There was giddy anticipation in the air of what that special day would hold. Once mom and dad left, the girls and I continued our morning. We soon left to hang out at North Park Mall so we could be close to the hospital their sister would be arriving at. To pass the time, we strolled around looking at storefronts, watched the turtles in an indoor pond, threw coins in the fountain, and ate lunch at Chick-fil-A. After we'd done all we could, it was time to head to the hospital.

As we arrived I quickly found that spaces were limited in the underground garage. It was the same weekend Hurricane Rita was expected to make landfall around Houston, so the hospitals in south Texas had evacuated north to Dallas. The hospital was busy and packed. Holding a hand of each girl, we walked into the hospital's women's building, rode the elevator to the proper floor, and were greeted by the girls' dad. He walked us down to a corner room where the grandparents, mother, and a brand-new baby sister were all staying. Before we entered, I quickly readied my camera so I could capture the moment. It was one of those moments you live for, and I wanted to make sure I captured every bit of it for this family.

With much anticipation, we entered. Two beautiful bright-eyed little girls meeting their squishy, peach-fuzzed, blue-eyed baby sister for the first time. The girls looked in wonder at this precious baby girl who was finally here—before their very eyes. They wanted to hug and hold and kiss but were not sure how. They each got a turn, and then all posed for their first picture together. Grandparents watched this wonderful family celebrate. Everything was as it should be.

The mother looked at me and asked if I'd like to hold her flannel-wrapped babe. I had no hesitation. She was warm and fit perfectly in the crook of my arm. I felt so comfortable; it felt so natural to hold her. I could have held that little girl the rest of the day, but eventually it was grandma's turn again so I handed her over.

I left the hospital feeling such peace about what I had witnessed. I wondered when it would be my turn, how many kids would I have, and how I'd do as a mother. I didn't let my thoughts linger, though. I figured motherhood wouldn't be anytime soon. I had just turned 20, we were barely making it financially, and I knew down deep that we just weren't ready.

Little did I know that this day would be the one I looked back on as a marker for the beginning of a new journey.

I had been on birth control since we were married. Using the handy chart my doctor gave me, I had chosen this new kind of pill in which, instead of your cycle being monthly, things would circle around every three months. I thought it was brilliant, and it seemed to work great for us.

Around the time of my employers having their third girl, I decided to stop taking my pill. I have never been able to put my finger on *why* I made this choice. I remember mentioning it to Bobby, about stopping, and all he said in response was, "OK, sure." That's all it took, and I never swallowed another pill. We were married, and I knew how babies were made, but I remember having such naive thoughts about my decision. I guess I simply thought I wouldn't get pregnant anytime soon.

Toward the end of October Bobby and I were set to go on a weekend conference with our friends. The night before I had trouble sleeping and began to toss and turn. During the night I noticed my chest was sore. Similar to when I would have my monthly cycle, but more so. This reminded me of how my boss knew she was pregnant again; she had experienced the same feelings with her girls. This thought made me wonder if . . . I might be pregnant too. It had been six weeks since my last monthly, but due to the type of birth control I was on, I knew it would take some time for my body to regulate. I didn't think this length of time was anything to take special note of.

The next morning, we woke up extra early to head out on our trip. I mentioned to Bobby the feelings I was experiencing. We agreed to keep this a secret and see how the weekend went. If I still hadn't started by the time we got home, I would take a pregnancy test.

As the weekend continued I found my hunger increasing. I had never experienced ravenous hunger quite like this. I began to have headaches, turn weak, then nauseous. As soon as I'd have some real edible substance, all these indications would fade away. There were times my eyes would become so heavy with tiredness it seemed there was no amount of noise that could keep me from fading to sleep.

With each symptom of pregnancy, I'd share with Bobby. He'd return with acknowledgments of sly winks, grins, and subtle back rubs. He would head to the concessions area and come back with all kinds of food. He did not want me to go hungry since I was possibly carrying our child!

We enjoyed that weekend more than we had anticipated. And we shared this small secret that appeared to display itself more and more as the trip went on. We were definitely getting excited, but also trying not to get our hopes up until we knew for sure.

I wasn't able to test until after the work day the following Monday. The evidence continued throughout the day, and I was anxious to get to the drug store. As I searched the aisle for pregnancy tests, I remembered a friend of mine advising me when I got married to be sure and get a certain type of test if I ever felt the need. These were digital and would not leave you guessing if you saw a line or not. I grabbed the box and headed to the register, handing the cashier my item while feeling a wave of heat rush over me. It hit me: the first person outside of our bubble knew! She was a stranger, but still she knew our secret. I held my head high to remind myself I was a married woman, and I strategically placed my hand so she could see my wedding bands!

I quickly drove the quarter-mile home and rushed up three flights of stairs to our apartment. Once inside, I thoroughly read the instructions. I sat down on the toilet and completed the test. Not looking, I set the stick down at my feet. I sat there staring at the wall waiting for the recommended minutes to pass. In a moment's time I felt this sense come over me that . . . life as I knew it would never be the same. As soon as that feeling hit, I took the courage to look down. The word "pregnant" presented itself on the screen.

I picked up the test to look closer, looked away, then back down at it to be sure I was reading correctly. I was. There was no denying. In an instant, I became nervous, as if I'd done something wrong. Quickly, I reminded myself that I was married and this was all OK . . . this was bound to happen at some point... surely, people would know this. My next thoughts quickly carried over into wondering how we'd be able to afford this baby. I didn't know but reminded myself to take this one step at a time. We'd have months, I told myself, to figure this out.

The first step was to tell Bobby. I called him, and he was finishing up work and driving by his parents' home to drop some things off. We had plans to do yard work around town that night to make some extra money, so I decided to meet him at his folks' place. I freshened up, grabbed my purse, the test, and left as quickly as I'd arrived. I didn't want to tell Bobby over the phone. He didn't even know I'd gone to the store yet.

When I pulled up, he was putting the remaining tools away in the barn. I noticed his parents' vehicles in the driveway. I put my old tan Toyota Corolla in park, rolled the window down, and sat there to watch as he finished up. Once he lowered the barn door, he walked over and asked how my day was.

I smiled and said, "It was good," then paused a moment and added, "I have something to show you."

I reached over, grabbed the gray and blue stick that had the word "pregnant" across the screen, and handed it to him. Smiling, Bobby took it. It was as though he just stood there studying the word.

Finally, he blurts out, "Is this real? How do you know it's right?"

With a smirk, I answered, "Well, it wouldn't be positive if I wasn't pregnant."

Again he asked: "Are you for real?"

"Yes."

Bobby opened the door, then leaned in for a long hug and kiss. We began laughing; we couldn't believe it. We were overwhelmed, but also excited, by what this meant. We were growing up. We were growing our family. We had no clue how, but we told ourselves we would figure it out one step at a time. Together.

I told Bobby I wanted to keep this to ourselves and that we'd tell our families once we finished with our work that night. He agreed.

We decided to ride together and take his truck. I hopped in, and Bobby mentioned he had to run inside to get something. He came back fairly quickly and we left. Here's what I didn't know: he had gone inside to tell his parents they were going to be grandparents.

We got through our yard work as quickly as we could. We were so excited and anxious to tell the people closest to us. After we finished up, we headed to my parents' house. As we headed up their gravel drive, the butterflies hit my stomach. I didn't expect anything other than happiness from them, but even though I was the oldest I was still very young. I just didn't know how they would react. We gathered my parents together and said we had something we needed to discuss.

I have found it's easier in these situations to get the news out fast! The buildup of anticipation seems to wreak havoc on my nerves; I can only assume it does for others as well.

So without further wait, I jumped in. "Umm . . . you're going to be grandparents."

My dad raised his eyebrows and just said, "Really?" Then he smiled. "Congratulations."

My mom's jaw dropped a little, she sort of smiled as if she had an inkling, and then she followed with a slew of questions: "How far along are you?" "When did you find out?" "Have you seen a doctor yet?" "Were you taking your pills?" "Who all have you told?"

I answered each one as best I could, and they were happy. We were sure we had done everything right, and there was to be another baby in the family. What's not to love? Their biggest concern likely was the reality of everything and how we would afford this baby, but they were genuinely delighted in the news.

We left with smiles and happy hearts as we headed to Bobby's parents. He called to make sure they were both there, as we had requested. But after Bobby hung up he told me he had a confession: he'd already told his parents.

My personality tends to want things "just so." I had built up this plan in my head as to how things should go, and Bobby's sneaky self took the plan into his own hands and ran with it. I was shocked. It took me a moment to be OK with it, but as we made our way across town we began to laugh. He was so eager; he just felt he couldn't contain himself when he told his parents the news earlier that evening. Bobby was going to be a dad. I couldn't deny him his happiness.

As we walked to their back door, the butterflies hit again. My in-laws already knew I was pregnant, but I had not yet seen them. I knew without any doubt they'd be happy. First, Bobby had told me their response from earlier; second, they had lived similar lives. They'd been together since the eighth grade, married a year after high school, and expected their first son, Bobby, after only three months of marriage.

We were greeted by both of his parents, who were thrilled about our family growing. Bobby's mom asked me the due date. I told her it looked to be about mid to late June. They started to reminisce about the beginning of their marriage, and how it was to bring home a new baby. They said it was hard trying to make it with a little one, but somehow they managed to make it work, and they obviously went on to have two more.

Seeing them smile about the past and looking at how far they had come assured us that if they could do it, we could too.

We would be just fine. We would figure this out together.

Three

One of the most important questions from my mother concerned my prenatal care. When would I be going to the doctor? This scared me because I'd never been to a doctor by myself! I had no clue about insurance, copays, things like this. I had been blessed to have my parents continue to cover me for medical insurance, but I was still lost in this department. Honestly, going by myself and figuring these details out seemed more "grown-up" than anything I had ever done. I only had Bobby and myself to worry about until now, but this was different. We had another being to care for now, one who would depend on us for everything.

Again, I was reminding myself to take things one step at a time . . . *Make the call* . . . *Set up an appointment.*

My first prenatal appointment was set up for an afternoon so I could work most of the day and get off early. When the day came for my appointment, I was about seven to eight weeks along. I got off early, just as planned, Bobby met me at our apartment, and we drove together to the OB-GYN. I began the process of checking in. The receptionist asked for my insurance card. I handed her what I thought she needed; it turned out it wasn't. It was a membership card from my insurance company, but apparently not the card you hand to medical professionals. I mentioned that it wasn't my first time with this doctor and that they should have everything on file. She looked, and sure enough they did. She checked the insurance they had for me from when I started birth control. It was still valid, but for whatever reason it wouldn't cover my pregnancy! The lady told me they would need five hundred dollars before we could start the appointment! I was . . . dumbfounded. Of course, I didn't have the money to pay that amount. I barely had the copay money! Sadly, we had to walk out before the appointment even began. I called my mom to let her know. She was just as surprised as I was, but sure enough, we found out the insurance I had wasn't going to work for prenatal care.

Now that I was married, my parents had taken a back seat to my decision-making. They wanted me to figure things out on my own and knew I was perfectly capable of doing so. For the most part, they trusted my judgment, so they didn't say much. So here I was, basically at a loss as to what to do. I did not know what to do next; that very thought seemed to overwhelm me. I sat on my hands for about two to three weeks before I took any action. Thankfully, the mother of the girls I took care of had extra prenatal vitamin samples her doctor gave her during her last pregnancy, and she had given them all to me. I knew they were important, so I began to take them.

Something we noticed soon after Bobby and I married is that we became, essentially, unrelatable with nearly everyone our age. Through Amway, a multilevel marketing company, we became friends with many people older than us. Most were married, and some had kids. One night we were out with some friends at a meeting. After it was over, everyone hung around and chatted. The men and women seemed to gather separately. The women started talking about having babies. Everyone knew I was expecting, and the usual questions about prenatal and delivery came up. I didn't have any answers for them. My friend mentioned she used a midwife at a birth center and said this was a lot less expensive than a hospital birth. This intrigued me. I wanted to know more. To me, an out-of-hospital birth and not using a doctor was like something taboo, something only crazy people would do. You weren't allowed medicine for pain and, at first thought, that seemed absurd. My friend was one of us, though. She was kind, gentle, and a true friend. She wasn't "crazy," she was real, and she was someone I respected. With several of the women listening, she went on to share her experience.

She talked about her prenatal visits and how relaxing they were. She would lay on a couch instead of a table. The midwives were invested in her care and that of her baby. They would listen to her feelings, concerns, and pay attention to the details of how her body was changing.

I was completely enthralled by her birth story and found myself hanging on every word. As she spoke about the delivery, everything seemed so peaceful despite the fact she hadn't taken any pain medication. She called it a "supernatural childbirth."

In that moment, listening to her every detail, I could feel it. This was how it was supposed to be. There was no other way. This was the answer. I knew it. Everything felt right.

I felt confident I could do this. I kept thinking back to my childhood. Whenever my mother felt I was being disrespectful or mouthy, she would remind me of what she went through to get me here: "Seven and a half hours of labor. No pain medication. Not *even* an aspirin." Though labor and delivery is obviously a painful experience, I knew that if my mom could handle it, I could too.

On the way home that night, I told Bobby what my friend had shared, how wonderful her experience was, and that it was less expensive than using a conventional doctor and hospital. He didn't have much of a response, but eventually said that if I felt this is what we should do, then he supported my decision.

I began my due diligence in search of a birth center and midwife. I looked at the center my friend delivered at; it was located in the heart of Dallas. Though less expensive than a hospital, it was still more than our budget could handle. I continued to search for others. At the time, there weren't many in the entire Dallas-Fort Worth area, especially on the east side of the metroplex. I found one that sparked my interest more than the others, but it was across the DFW metroplex and took about seventy-five to ninety minutes to reach. Just outside Weatherford is the humble little town of Peaster. In that quiet little town was a birth center that sat on a horse farm. Simple, quaint, perfect. The price was also unmatched by any other location in the area. I called and the appointment was made. The woman I spoke with told me to bring my list of questions, and they would be sure to answer them.

At about twelve weeks along, during the Christmas and

New Year's holidays, my free consultation appointment was scheduled. Bobby had to work, so he wasn't able to make it. I made the long trek across the metroplex area, and beyond, by myself. I tend to enjoy some "me time," so that aspect didn't bother me, but being that we were talking about our first child, I wanted Bobby there. He is the ultimate decision-maker in our home, and this didn't seem like something I should decide on my own. At least, I didn't want to make these important decisions on my own.

In hindsight, Bobby didn't know the first thing about pregnancy and babies. The idea of it all was so foreign to him.

As soon as I arrived, I was introduced to the head midwife/owner and her two apprentices. They sat me down, along with another couple, to watch a documentary about a natural, unmedicated childbirth. The movie followed the story of a midwife in Mexico having an unassisted home birth. It started out with her in the early stages of labor and going on with life as normal. She sat down to eat dinner with her large, extended family, but somewhere in the course of her meal she decided she couldn't stay at the table; things were getting uncomfortable just sitting there. She began to wander around. Her husband was always nearby. At one point the video showed her dancing or swaying back and forth with him as she hummed to drown out the pain.

Watching, I reminded myself there were still a lot of people in the home going about their business. The woman eventually got into a big tub. It was more like a hot tub lined with the most beautiful hand-painted tiles. She was completely exposed while laboring in the water. Her husband and one of her older children joined her in the water. The baby was soon born, and everyone was in total bliss—just as any birth of a baby should be—and all this without seemingly any care that they were basically swimming in a tub! I had seen the show "A Baby Story" on TLC, so I thought I knew what birth was like—but this was a whole new level of *raw*. I had never seen anything quite like this. I wondered what I had gotten myself into.

I quickly glanced over at the husband also watching the video. His wife was all smiles, but he had a blank stare across his face and was as still as could be. I was uncomfortable for him and was so glad Bobby wasn't there. Bobby wouldn't have been able to sit through the video without voicing his thoughts. He would have been mortified and checked out of the whole process from the beginning.

After the documentary the owner began to show us around the birth center. She started with the prenatal room where they held exams. Then the kitchen; she said we could eat during labor and have someone cook or heat food if needed. Then we moved down the hallway to the birthing rooms.

She explained the birthing tub and the process of delivering in it. There was a window above the tub, and she mentioned how several babies had been born by moonlight and/or candlelight in that very spot. She went on to talk about how a mother in labor is treated as a queen—she even has the final word on the thermostat. I began to cherish this way of care and birthing. It felt like a dream—despite the looming physical pain involved. It felt right, just as birth is intended to be.

I remember seeing several framed black and white pictures displayed as a timeline of a pregnant woman in one of the hallways. They shared how each picture was a self-portrait taken every month of her pregnancy; the last one was taken while in labor. I thought they were the coolest things, showing her body flourish as she grew another human being. This woman was a birth photographer the business worked with often, and also was a client. The photos on the wall held special meaning to the midwife. Later, I would look at her works in awe, hoping and praying to have the chance to experience what the women in her photographs went through in those moments.

To capture a new life being born in all its messy glory is such a breathtaking miracle. A treasure that my heart desired.

As we made our way back to the prenatal room, the midwives asked if I'd like to hear my baby's heartbeat. Since I was about twelve weeks along, they knew there was great possibility of hearing it. Of course I wanted to hear it, but Bobby wasn't there and it concerned me to experience this first one without him. I called to make sure it was OK with him, and it was. Looking back, this was such a minute thing to be concerned about, but it seemed so big at the time. They had me lie down and lift my shirt to show my belly. One of the apprentice midwives, Kelly, squirted the cool jelly on my stomach and began moving the wand of the doppler around the lower part of my abdomen. You could hear the waves of static as she glided over my tummy. Finally, we could hear what sounded like a horse running at full speed. We all lit up with smiles and giggles—we could hear the life of another being inside of me. I got out my phone to record the sound so I could share with Bobby and the rest of our family. One hundred and fifty-six beats per minute: a strong, healthy heartbeat. In that moment, I became overwhelmed with happiness and a feeling of completion. I couldn't wait for Bobby to hear the sound of our child's heartbeat so he could be just as delighted as I was.

Next we moved to the waiting room where we had first watched the documentary. We sat on couches the head midwife and owner, asked if I had any questions. I grinned a bit sheepishly and pulled out my list. She chuckled a little and said, "No one has ever brought an actual list of questions." I replied, "Well you told me to be sure and bring a list of questions." We all had a good laugh about this, but I felt they were actually impressed with my diligence. They respected every question I had and answered each one. They had probably been asked these same questions a hundred times or more, but the women carried so much care and compassion for what they did that it felt like I was the first person to share these thoughts. More and more I felt my concerns slip away, like layers being peeled from an onion, and I felt at peace. This was the way for me.

Once we finished the student midwife asked if I liked what I saw and what they had to offer. I told her I did, but that I had to talk to my husband to make sure. She nodded. I told her I'd call as soon as we had.

I climbed into the truck and immediately called Bobby to ramble on about the visit and everything I was feeling. Eventually, I asked if I should make this our choice. I felt dumbfound by his response: "It's up to you. You did the research and you're the one who was just there. It's your decision. . . . What do you want to do?" I felt barely qualified to make such a judgment regarding medical care, but he trusted my call and left the choice to me. Ultimately, it was freeing. I had this epiphany kind of moment in which I felt truly capable of deciding the best route for our baby and myself. I called them back shortly afterward and set up our first official prenatal appointment for just after the new year.

We began to tell others what I had decided—a midwife and delivering at a birth center. Some were ecstatic, some were curious, some were leery, and some were downright against this choice. We learned early on to keep this decision to ourselves unless we were asked or were around people who delighted in the idea of this unique way of doing things. In all fairness to the naysayers, I understood the depth of their concerns and the risks involved, but deep down I knew this was where I was supposed to be.

It was a chilly day in January 2009. Bobby was able to make it to my first official prenatal appointment. I was about fifteen weeks along at this point and getting past the questionable stage between looking fat or looking pregnant. I introduced Bobby to the midwives.

Kelly, an apprentice assigned to me during her studies, shook Bobby's hand and asked, "Did you bring your catcher's mitt?"

Confused, Bobby could only blurt out, "What do you mean?"

I snickered as I knew what she was hinting at.

Grinning, Kelly replied, "To catch your baby, of course."

Bobby was taken back. "No, ma'am. I'm going to be in the kitchen cooking up meals."

At this point I lost it; his response was golden. I guess when I told him about the consultation appointment, the kitchen part is what stuck with him. Pope men are known for their expert cooking skills, so he probably figured the kitchen would be where he could help out. Cooking whatever I wanted.

Kelly responded, "Umm . . . no, Daddy. You are going to stay right with your wife and help her wherever she needs you. Chances are that's not going to be in the kitchen."

We all had a good laugh at that introduction and continued with the appointment. They gave another quick tour of the center to catch Bobby up on what he missed, and then they went on with the usual prenatal routines: weighing, peeing, checking blood pressure, listening to the baby's heartbeat, and going through a list of questions about my progress and any symptoms I may have had.

I enjoyed and looked forward to my appointments with these ladies. Every time I walked away with more knowledge than I entered with. I was amazed at the entire process my body was going through. Their passion was contagious, and I didn't mind catching it. Every time, it felt like Bobby and I were in the presence of God; we could just *feel* that everything was as it should be. It was common for my appointment to last an hour or so. I'm not talking about showing up and waiting for it to start and then leaving one hour after entering; the *actual time* spent with these ladies lasted sixty minutes. It was a different kind, almost a different level, of care than I had never experienced or heard of.

Toward the end of March, I had my first sonogram appointment. I was just past twenty weeks. This is the time an in-depth sonogram is usually done, checking every vital thing from head to toe, and possibly finding out the baby's gender. We went to White Rose Women's Center in Dallas, right off of Interstate 75. My checkup was set for an evening appointment. Traffic was horrific; it was rush hour. Bobby and I planned to meet there with our mothers. I was running late and Bobby was running extra late. This stressed me out. We finally got there and all filed into the exam room. They had the blinds closed to darken the windows; a huge TV monitor hooked up to their machine showed everything they were seeing as they looked, allowing us to watch it as well.

The appointment went smoothly. My stress faded when

we saw our baby moving. The sweet profile picture, precious hands and feet, were all a sight to see. We watched as the sonographer took her time studying every detail. Our baby measured about a week behind, but she assured us this was still within normal range. Everything appeared perfect. We wanted to know the gender; she shared that we were having a boy. We were elated.

A baby boy. I was happy to know this huge detail about God's gift to me. I didn't know anything about this little fellow except for his heartbeat—until this day. My mind could finally begin imagining what life would be like. I hadn't been around little boys much, so I could only go on what people had told me about them. I was eager to be this boy's mama and looking forward to watching him grow. I took time to contemplate what this news meant for every family member in the room.

Bobby was super enthusiastic and voiced his extreme happiness. To say he was relieved we weren't having a girl was an understatement. Since he grew up being the oldest of all boys, he didn't know the first thing about little girls—and frankly he didn't care to know. The thought of changing a girl's diaper disturbed him. To Bobby, we would only have boys . . . like we could really control this. I knew he was misguided and believed God would correct his view of raising a girl someday. I still loved him and knew he'd be an awesome father despite these thoughts.

His mom, Michele, was giddy. Though I know she may have wanted a little girl, she was warmed by the thought of another boy. A boy can be quite rambunctious—imagine the thought of one being Bobby's son—but we all knew boys were sweet and had the ability to melt you like butter.

Then, my mom. I was completely delighted for her. Not because she was a mother of girls, but that she also had a baby boy waiting for her in Heaven. My brother passed away at only three days old, on Thanksgiving Day; he had an undetected heart defect. I was about ten at the time. She never got to raise this son, so in one very real sense, this was an answer to her desire for a little boy. My family would finally get a little boy.

We had a predetermined name for this son. This was something that I had agreed to back when I was a sophomore in high school! Bobby's Grandma Pope took me aside at a youth event to tell me she had something very serious to discuss with me. She told me how she knew Bobby and I were pretty serious, and she knew how her grandson felt about me. Bobby, or Trey, is actually Bobby Lynn Pope III. He is named after his dad and grandpa. Grandma Pope wanted to make sure this tradition continued down to our firstborn son. When she asked this, I didn't hesitate. All three of these people she wanted my future child named for were good, godly men. Why wouldn't I want a son named after them? I agreed, and she insisted we shake on it and even had someone take our picture as proof.

This little boy was to be named Bobby Lynn Pope IV.

Four

I was well on my way to the third trimester. Baby showers were in the works, as was registering for baby items and lingering in the baby section at stores so I could adore the tiny clothing. Thoughts of childcare and pediatricians bounced in my head, and I watched my entire body begin to change.

One day after a shower I lathered lotion on my body as usual, but then noticed something I hoped to never see: stretchmarks. They weren't on my stomach at all, but were down my inner thighs and other places. Taking a closer look at my legs, I noticed the beginning of these marks appearing on my calves as well. This devastated me; they seemed to appear overnight, without warning. I used to be proud of my toned, petite body, but it had changed so much. There was nowhere for any extra weight to go, except out, and it really affected the way I looked. My midwives noticed this as well and had me start journaling the food I was eating. They gave me lists of healthy foods I should stick to and foods to stay away from and told me how much water and protein intake I should strive for every day. They also gave me a list of supplements they recommended. Despite how hard it could be, I did my best to do what they asked.

Bobby's family had property in Oklahoma. It was only about two and a half hours away, so we often found ourselves spending weekends there. It was not far west from Beaver's Bend and the Broken Bow area, so occasionally we would travel a little farther east to go trout fishing. Usually, I loved trout fishing. We would stop at a local hole-in-the-wall bait shop to get our fishing license and stock up on supplies. We would buy the little jars filled with brightly colored, slimy, squishy balls of bait and extra hooks. We had not mastered fly fishing, so we used ultralight rods and reels. My favorite part of the whole trout fishing experience was wearing waders and standing in the water without getting wet. Well, you had to be extra careful not to get wet. The stones in the water can be slippery, so if you aren't sure-footed, you can topple, filling your waders with water, and then you are soaked. We would go fishing here in late winter and early spring, so the water was *cold*.

I wasn't particularly good at catching trout. I could bait my hook like a champ, but caught many "tree bass" from over-casting, and I would only catch one or two trout when everyone else caught their limit. Despite my lack of success, trout fishing had become one of my favorite experiences in life. It was not the catching that made it fun; clearly that did not happen often. This part of Oklahoma is breathtaking, the water is clear, there are mountains in view, the trees are vast and many, and you enjoy time with family and friends making memories.

As we had done the past few years, in the early spring we took a trip east of our family's land to go trout fishing. This time, however, was different. Due to my growing body, I could not experience fishing the same as I had in the past. I could not fit in my waders like before; I could not even get a leg in! I had to stick to the shore, where it was even *harder* to not hook a tree. Everyone would move to different spots if they weren't getting bites. This is just the nature of fishing. It is a lot easier when you are not limited to sticking to land, though. There were huge rocks and boulders along the shore, which made it hard for a pregnant woman to travel down the bank. I eventually found myself alone and frustrated with fishing. Once everyone had drifted out of sight, I sat down and let my pregnancy hormones overtake me. I cried . . . a lot. Trout fishing had become one of my favorite things in the whole world—and now it wasn't. I didn't care that I couldn't actually fish. I wanted to at least watch the others as they did, but even that wasn't possible. Though I wanted to stay with everyone, I didn't want to hinder their fishing by making them feel they had to stay back for my sake.

I sat there for some time just sorting through my emotional thoughts. Though I did not like the way this pregnancy made me feel encumbered, I reminded myself I was growing something special. Making the most of my situation, I took this time alone in God's creation to pray to Him about my feelings and pray over my baby. After a bit, I was able to gather my sentiments and compose myself.

Eventually, members of our fishing crew returned and my cares faded. I was relieved to be in their presence again, hear their stories, and see how many fish they had caught. I was also relieved because I knew it meant we would be eating soon! Since I was eating for two, I was quite ready for a meal!

I didn't like the situation I found myself in that day, but in the end it was good for me. I was alone in nature, and the only thing I could do was be still and pray. It is a memory that has remained with me.

Since the beginning of the pregnancy, Bobby had started a business of providing firewood to barbeque restaurants. He had permission to harvest trees from a man's property in Texas, and his parents had given him permission to take some trees from their property in Oklahoma. If the days worked well allowing that I could go with him to Oklahoma, I would. It was April now, and the reality had set in that any kind of physical work alongside Bobby was now out of the question. I still went to help where I could, and, if anything, to keep him company.

It was Easter weekend, which meant I had four days off. We decided to leave Thursday evening so Bobby would have a full day's work on Friday gathering wood. We spent the night at his parents' cabin, which they had built. It wasn't anything fancy, but it was something to be proud of—a family effort. The piers were old telephone poles and the floor was made of ply-wood. We had reused wood siding from an old apartment complex for the outside of the walls, and the roof was good old-fashioned corrugated metal. The porch spanned the width of the structure and the posts were trunks of cedar trees we had found on the property. There was no electricity, running water, or insulation. We used an antique potbelly stove to heat up the place in the colder months. Since we visited this place on weekends, we got our fill of the primitive, pioneer lifestyle without having to be fully committed to it.

I had never spent a night in that cabin with just Bobby and me—until that night. Every bed and cot were usually filled with some family member, and any outdoor sounds were usually muffled by someone rustling around the cabin. But with just the two of us, this night was different. It was quite chilly, so we slept bundled together as close as we could to the stove for warmth without being too close (and thus placing ourselves in danger). Everything produced a different sound than I had experienced before. It made me think of a scene right out of a classic novel.

At night, when Laura lay awake in the trundle bed,
she listened and could not hear anything at all but
the sound of the trees whispering together.
—LAURA INGALLS WILDER, LITTLE HOUSE IN THE BIG WOODS[1]

We woke up by the light of the sunrise the next morning and ate breakfast with what was available in the cabin. There was not anything in that meal that my midwives recommended, but it filled us up and we were able to get moving for the day. Bobby worked all day to fill the orders he promised he would meet. I rode along with him around the property as he worked. He found a task I was capable of handling. It wasn't anything too crazy, but it was enough to cut a little time off his work. He placed a seat for me right next to his log splitter. I worked the lever that controls the hydraulics for the splitter to move up and down as it split the logs. All Bobby had to do was put a new log on, let it split, and take it off. We did this the entire day, stopping to eat snacks in the cabin when we'd get hungry.

Toward the end of the day it became apparent we would have to stay another night. Bobby hadn't collected enough wood to fill his orders. I didn't want to stay another night. We had a birthing class, conveniently followed by a prenatal checkup, scheduled for the next day, Saturday the 11th.

We came back to the cabin to get refueled again and work through our plans. In the heat of the discussion of whether we should stay or go, I told Bobby I had not felt any significant baby kicks since Wednesday night. I distinctly remember waking to use the restroom in the middle of the night and feeling our baby kick like crazy. Since that night, I had felt movement, but it was more of a shifting and not the powerful little kicks or jabs. Since I still felt movement, it did not concern me as much, but as time went on anxiety began to creep in. I kept all this to myself for a while, thinking it was probably nothing. Sometimes I would pray over the child to rid my negative thoughts. This prayer conversation broke me, forcing me to spill my worries to Bobby.

The news derailed our conversation and shifted our mood. A look of confusion came over Bobby and he asked, "What do you mean?" I replied, "I have felt some movement, but not like I used to. Not any kicks, or anything like that, for a couple days now. I've just been praying and trying to think positively. I mean, I still feel like I feel something every now and again." I paused. "I am just ready to get back home so we can make it to Weatherford in time." Bobby took that moment to lay his hands on my stomach and pray over our baby. His prayer gave me enough peace to keep going.

He made a plan for us to leave extra early in the morning so we could make our appointments on time. He worked until night fell and he couldn't see anymore, and then we went to bed.

When morning arrived, my alarm woke me. I noticed the empty space next to me in bed and looked up to spot Bobby through the window loading the remaining wood on the trailer. The air was crisp and I could see the sun's light barely peaking above the trees behind him; this bit of light showed his breath billowing out as steam. I put on a jacket, slid my boots on, and walked out to greet him and see how much more he had to load. He had been up since before dawn, he said, and was just finishing his load. He asked if I would gather his things so we could be on our way. Not long after, we were loaded and ready to go.

Bobby asked if I could drive so he could catch up on sleep. We had a long goosenecked trailer attached, but I didn't mind. I knew to take wide turns and not get in too much of a hurry. We stopped at the Choctaw travel center just south of Hugo, Oklahoma to fill up on gas and grab some breakfast to eat while traveling. I drove the entire way home as Bobby slept.

Once we got home, we quickly showered and were out the door again. The only thing I had clean to wear were some red and white plaid PJs and an old shirt. My hair was wet; I didn't have time to dry it. As much as we had tried to do it all, we still found ourselves running late. I called my midwife and told her we were running late and would be there as soon as possible.

Sure enough, we arrived late and she had already started the class. We quietly took a seat as she introduced us to the others. There were two other couples attending the class that day. In great detail, the midwife went through the entire process of how a baby is born and what to expect. Some of it was review, but a lot of it was new information. She showed us different techniques used to relieve pain and help with coping through the entire labor and delivery process.

Once the birthing class was over and the other expecting couples left, we headed to our prenatal appointment. Weighing myself and peeing in a cup to dip a multicolored strip in were done first; this had become routine with these appointments. We talked about my diet and I shared my journal. It was then that I shared I had not felt any significant kicks since Wednesday night. They did not appear to be crazy concerned by this news, but looking back I'm sure they were just trying to keep it together for my sake.

Still, everything seemed to check out well. We moved into the exam room where they would check my blood pressure, measure my fundal height, and listen for the baby's heartbeat. When they measured my fundal height to see how big my uterus was, they found I was measuring about a week or two behind. They took note of this and we moved on to the next thing, the doppler. Kelly first felt around over my stomach, feeling for the baby to get her bearings for where to place the wand. She showed me where his head was and let me feel. It was so crazy; I could actually place my hand to feel his head, down his back, and to his bottom. She placed the doppler where she figured his heart was, expecting to immediately hear it beating, but we only heard static. She tried a few more times and even took turns with other midwives there. Occasionally we would hear a sound that resembled a baby moving, but we could never catch a heartbeat.

After a few moments the head midwife, suggested we go to another birth center with a sonogram machine to see if we could get a better check on our baby; she directed one of the others to call a center in Grand Prairie. She picked that one because it would be on our way home. She asked if I was OK with this, and my biggest concern was money: would it cost anything? She assured me it wouldn't. I smiled and just felt happy I would get to see and hear my baby again. It hadn't occurred to me what they were actually thinking and concerned about.

Kelly offered to meet us at the center. Since we were her case study, she wanted to be with us.

I was looking forward to seeing my baby again.

Bobby and I left and made a stop at the first fast-food place we saw, Dairy Queen. It was now mid-afternoon and we were both hungry. I remember ordering this orange smoothie thing. It was a soft serve ice cream drink mixed with orange sherbet; a high school drill team friend had introduced me to this concoction. It tasted just like an orange push-pop. I sucked it down, leaned the passenger chair back, and went to sleep as Bobby drove.

I woke up to the movement of the car turning, which indicated to me we had exited the interstate and were getting close to the other birthing center. I noticed the sun would be setting soon as even the car's visor couldn't keep the sun from shining in my eyes. What a day this had been to this point.

We pulled into the center's parking lot. The building was probably about a hundred years old and was once a two-story house. It was one of those homes that had to have held a great deal of history, and it made me wonder about life "back in the day." We arrived before Kelly and noticed other people there, so we went in. The midwives greeted us. They were very young ladies, much like myself. I figured they couldn't have been more than a year or two older than me. They wore long skirts and small white head coverings. They didn't say much, which made the initial moments a little awkward. I tried to break the silence by complimenting them on their facility, but all I got in return was a quick thank you. I still had not realized the weight of the situation. They, I believe now, did.

Kelly soon arrived. I was relieved to see her. We made small talk about what we ate on the way. When she heard what I had to drink, she asked if I noticed any movement. Since the drink was filled with sugar, she was thinking I should probably have felt something. I had fallen asleep right after I finished the drink, so if there was movement, I didn't know it. She nodded and suggested we go upstairs to have a look.

We followed the other midwives up the stairs and down the hall, peeking in the birth rooms as we passed. We entered the last room on the right and they asked me to lie down on the other side of a queen size bed; they rolled an ancient sonography machine close. This machine had to have been about twenty years old. The screen was so tiny and the whole thing had that antique colored look to it. I lifted my shirt, they turned on the machine, squirted the gel on my stomach, and began looking.

In a moment we saw my still, lifeless baby. No heartbeat. A huge wave of anxiety rushed over my body as reality set in. The other midwives looked at Kelly and shook their heads "no." In that moment, Kelly spoke to me in a gentle, motherly tone. "Sweetie, your baby has passed. There is no heartbeat." She went on to explain what they had been looking at. "There should be a flutter on the screen, and there is not." The others pointed to his heart, and it had no beat.

Sadness was all around me as I tried to process the news. Bobby, who was standing on the other side of the bed, climbed over and wrapped his arms around me. I covered my face to hold back tears I could not control. There was an emptiness in the depths of my being. Everyone cleared the room except for Kelly and Bobby. Kelly came around to my side of the bed, got down on my level, and spoke to me. I faintly remember her taking the time to pray over us. She briefly talked about options, then recommended we take some time to rest, think, and pray about what to do next. She encouraged us to gather our things and let us know she would be with us every step of the way and would be in touch soon.

Passing the other birth rooms again, I turned to look in each one and could feel nothing but unfairness at my situation. *How could this happen?* Time slowed to a crawl. My bones and muscles ached; I was weak from emotional pain. My eyes focused, like tunnel vision, as I tried to process what had just happened.

We passed the other midwives on our way out and told them thank you. I realized they had stopped whatever they were doing that day to help another midwife deliver wrenchingly difficult news to her client. There was no expectation for compensation. Like being part of an unspoken sisterhood, they always had each other's backs . . . this was something I was beginning to learn about this community of women. They felt the need to serve mothers wholeheartedly and passionately, no matter whose client it was.

Five

We left the birth center in silence. Bobby and I attempted to work through our thoughts before we shared them with each other. Bobby held it together, for the most part, while we were with others. I gathered my feelings the best I could. It was hard. We drove this way for a time, but eventually we could not hold it in any longer.

I felt embarrassment and remember feeling shallow for having this emotion. I was only a couple years out of high school, so I still had young adult tendencies in that I often cared too much about what others thought of me. I was aware of this: I would be a conversation piece for others in one of the saddest ways possible. Sadness—it was something I didn't want to be associated with . . .

I had a flashback to fifth grade, when I returned to school after my baby brother died. My parents had kept me out of school for a few days, not having me return until after his funeral. I arrived at school a few minutes after the bell rang for the day's start. I walked myself through the school and down the fifth-grade hallway. In those days teachers left their classroom doors open. As I passed each classroom, I could see my peers and they could see me. I distinctly remember other students staring and whispering—"She's here . . . She's back"—and pointing at me. I finally entered my classroom, and while everyone was extra nice, they also didn't know how to act around me. It was almost like I was the new kid. Eventually, things returned to normal, but I never forgot the sinking feeling of being the center of everyone's attention . . .

A wave of grief rushed over me and I began to wail uncontrollably. I yelled: *"Why?! Why me?!"* I just wanted my baby. I felt as if someone had stolen him from us. It wasn't fair. Bobby put his hand on me as he drove.

We realized we needed to tell people and wondered how someone delivers such news. Bobby's parents were out of town, so calling them was our only option. We called and talked briefly. We gave them the news, answered their questions, hoped for a miracle, and ended in prayer. As horrible as the news was, we were calm when we hung up. I had decided this news was too much for a phone call to my parents, so we decided to go straight to their house from the birth center.

We called my parents to make sure they were home and mentioned we had something to tell them. I'm sure they sensed something wasn't right. We arrived, found both of them, and broke the news. This pain was all too familiar for them, but they stayed rather reserved. I'm sure they felt the need to be strong for their daughter and son-in-law. We mostly kept it together ourselves, but I had a few tears drop from my eyes; my lip quivered a few times. I distinctly remember my mother looking me in the eyes and telling me one of the best pieces of advice she ever gave me. Sadly, she was dispensing that advice from personal experience. She looked at me and said, "Do not take anything to dull the pain you are feeling. I know it is and will be hard to deal with, but you are going to want to remember everything. If someone offers you medication, don't take it. You will want these memories someday. Trust me." She spoke with so much loving authority it was as if God was speaking through her, saying, "Child, I need you to remember the details." I knew I had to not rush through even the most mundane of activities so I could keep my memories. I vowed to myself that I would let it all soak in.

We did not stay long as we were worn out from the last couple of days and this immense burden. We knew it would be good for us to go home and catch up on sleep. We were ready to be home, but as tired as we were, we also found we could not rest. We could barely eat or sleep, and so we cried. We would cry until we thought we couldn't weep anymore. We'd take a breath and then crash into another wave of sorrow. Bobby and I were an emotional mess. It was like we would take turns . . . When I would go ballistic with my emotions, Bobby was the collected one and would comfort me. A little while later it would be his turn. He would lose it and just swim in his tears, and I would be the one holding it together to bring him back to peace. At other times, we were both in the depths of pain together. It hurt to cry, but we couldn't control ourselves. It was like we had no choice but to help one another get through this deep, sorrowful ache. We would replay the events leading to this point and try to will ourselves to wake from this nightmare. Prayer seemed to bring us comfort for a time, but our thoughts would get the best of us and we would be smashed with another wave of grief.

Somehow, we eventually worked our way out of it.

Kelly called to let me know she sent an email explaining our options. We could have an out-of-hospital birth at a center or in our home or decide to go the hospital route. Kelly said there were pros and cons with any of these choices, and she would do her best to give us all the information we needed to make the decision that was right for us. She assured us there is no right or wrong way to go through this and recommended we pray about it, talk to our family, ask any questions we might have, and then make the choice that was best for us; things weren't exactly an emergency. My initial feeling was to continue with an out-of-hospital birth at the birth center because it seemed peaceful and freeing, especially considering the circumstances. It was also what I had grown to set my heart on, and even though I wasn't going to bring my baby home, I did not want the birth experience robbed from me as well. We didn't make a final decision that night; we did not want to jump to any decision too quickly.

Eventually, we were tired enough that we felt we could actually get some sleep. Bobby fell asleep before me, and I lay there in the stillness of the night staring at the streetlight between the horizontal slats of our apartment blinds . . .

I felt I had just closed my eyes when I realized morning had come. I woke to the sound of the radio playing for our alarm. It was set to one of Dallas' local Christian radio stations. It was

Easter Sunday, April 12, 2009, and the radio greeted me with the beauty of the music and words of the Chris Tomlin song, "How Great Is Our God." Those five words are the heart of the song, and they hit me powerfully.

Lying there, my mind still hadn't returned to the news we had been slammed with the day before. When I heard the words to that song, I smiled; I had long wanted to sing it to my kids as a lullaby. I had a picture of them learning the words and singing it with me as I rocked them to sleep. But then . . . it did not take long for that sharp sword of pain to strike again, drowning my emotions as I was reminded of our harsh reality. Bobby tried to comfort me, but ultimately he ended up joining me and we wallowed in our emptiness again.

This day was an extremely tender day for us. It was Resurrection Day, we were dealing with our news, and it was the one year anniversary of Bobby's cousin Chynna's passing. She was a freshman when I was a senior in high school. We were both on the same drill team. In our lineup I was an end girl on the far right facing the audience, and Chynna was to my left. We grew close during my senior year. I would pick her up from her home and take her to church with me on Wednesday nights, we roomed together on our drill team's trip to Disney World, and she joined me at summer church camp. Once I got married and moved away, we weren't as close, but we would see each other at family gatherings on holidays and welcome each other with open arms, picking up right where we left off.

In the spring of 2008 it was discovered Chynna had a previously undetected heart defect. Once discovered, it was pressing that she have surgery right away; her heart was weak and couldn't handle much more. Naturally, this was a shock to everyone. She had danced her entire life, never missing an event, and had recently tried out to be the school's mascot—a jackrabbit—for her senior year of high school; she won that role. On Tuesday, April 8, 2008, Chynna entered the hospital for open heart surgery. The doctors appeared confident the surgery was going to be relatively easy and predicted Chynna would make it through with flying colors.

That evening, we received word she was still in surgery, and everyone in the extended family arrived for support. I didn't know the severity of Chynna's situation, that things were looking progressively grim. For the most part, everyone waiting had high hopes. Bobby's family is huge, and when he and I showed up at the hospital, the halls were lined with cousins sitting on the floor. We found the waiting room, but it was simply too cramped, so we took a spot on the floor in the hall with the rest of the family. We stayed a while, telling stories, and even heard a nurse give an update, but Chynna was taken back into surgery and it was getting late. Eventually, we had to leave as we both had work the next morning. Twenty-two hours later, from an operation that was supposed to last only four hours, Chynna was rolled out of the operating room.

She stayed in intensive care for four days until a doctor announced her passing. Chynna never woke from her surgery. Nothing was as it seemed. We were told her heart had been so weak it was like that of a 90-year-old woman, and that it was as thin as tissue paper. April 12, 2008 was recorded as the day Chynna Nicole Zmolik was welcomed into the arms of Jesus, just shy of her seventeenth birthday. Only about two weeks before her diagnosis, she had made the decision to give her life wholeheartedly to Christ. This was something I figured she had already done, seeing the way she always cared for people, but it was still heartwarming to hear this news. Despite the condition of her physical heart, her spiritual heart was made of gold, and it rubbed off on everyone she came in contact with. Our town's high school decided to close the doors the day of her funeral so students could attend and mourn together. She was—and still is—greatly missed. Never again this side of Heaven will I get to see her perfect smile with her Marilyn Monroe freckle above her lip, hear her infectious laugh and goofy noises, or see her boot-scoot across a stage, football field, or dance floor at another Zmolik wedding. She was everyone's favorite and always livened a room.

I share Chynna's story in such detail to say this: as Bobby and I entered the hospital on that first day of Chynna's time there and united with family in the halls, a feeling struck me. It was similar to a pregnant mother knowing whether she is carrying a boy or a girl before she is officially given the gender—that mother is confident in her instinct. I had this sense that it was going to be my turn in a year. What I mean is this: family was going to come line the halls of a hospital because I would be delivering a baby. Here's the catch: I was not pregnant, nor was I considering having a baby anytime soon. At the time I felt it odd that I had that thought . . . now, here I was a year later. I was pregnant and had just been told my baby's heart was no longer beating.

People would inevitably line the halls once again. Not to happily welcome a baby, but to mourn the loss of another life.

We considered staying home on that Easter Sunday. People would have understood, but we knew it would be harder on us if we did not get out and surround ourselves with people who love us. So we got dressed and went to church. During song service, we approached the pastor and asked for prayer, telling him our sad news. He prayed. Bobby and I were in constant prayer the entire time. It was like we were trying to will our baby to move, waiting on pins and needles to feel him kick. Bobby kept his hand on my stomach the whole time. We wanted so badly for this nightmare to be over and our baby to be miraculously raised from the dead. If God wanted to work a miracle such as this, wouldn't it be at a church service? That seemed to be our thinking.

It wasn't His will, however.

The rest of the day was a blur. We asked our families' opinions on our options, though my mind was already made up. That evening we spoke with Kelly and told her the route we had chosen for delivery. I still wanted to deliver at the birth center. She explained that with that choice I would have to have a professional sonogram again to check on everything inside my womb and allow them to see what we were working with.

Kelly was able to make an appointment for Wednesday, April 15 with the sonographer at White Rose Women's Center. Yes, I had to wait a few days, but I did not mind. I still had my baby, which meant God had a chance to miraculously heal him. Kelly met us at the women's center. Everything looked about as they expected for a baby who had not been alive in the womb for nearly a week. He was smaller; his skull's plates had started to cave, making him appear to have a bit of a cone shape to his head. The placenta was still intact but had started to peel away at the edges. We asked the sonographer if she felt that was the cause of death and she said no; the peeling was likely the beginning of deterioration. There was no sign showing the cause of death. There simply was no heartbeat and the signs of nature taking its course were evident.

Once the sonogram was over, Kelly took Bobby and I into a room with a small table and chairs. She needed to draw some blood samples for testing and discuss our options once more. Kelly explained delivering away from the hospital and the reality of what that looked like. Since there is no induction process in that way, we did not know when my body would go into labor. It could be another week or it could be a month; there was no way to tell. The longer we waited, we were told, the likelihood of an infection setting in increased. My baby's body would become more fragile the longer I carried him inside me.

The explanation of what his body would be like the longer we waited was so morbid this reality changed my mind. I no longer wanted a birth at the birth center. I wanted to deliver in the hospital and as soon as we could. The sonogram showed the beginnings of his body changing, and I did not want things to get worse.

Kelly was relieved when I expressed my change of heart. She suggested we deliver at Parkland Hospital. Cesareans had been on the rise in the DFW area, and she knew my chances of receiving one there would be lower since it was a state hospital. Kelly recommended we wait to check in until the next morning; this way we would be rested and have a fresh start to the day. She had already done some prework and called ahead to get details on the logistics since I had not seen a doctor or been to a clinic associated with Parkland. Even though I still wanted to give birth at the birthing center, there was a sense of peace that came over me after I made the decision to deliver in a hospital.

I know there are people who probably thought I was absolutely nuts for even considering an alternative to a hospital setting. Honestly, I would have felt the same before I started down the pregnancy road. But there is something about the type of care a midwife gives that draws a mother in. They treat you as if you are the only mother they are concerned with; they pay close attention to every detail. You are on a first-name basis. They will greet you with a smile and a hug, pray for you, and squeeze you tight when it's time to depart. I had felt this compassion from the birth center, and I did not want to lose it.

Kelly assured us that even though we decided to deliver in a hospital, she would be by our side every step of the way. I asked if she had ever experienced something like this. When she answered, I began to realize how deep and sincere her heart was for Bobby and me. She knew exactly what we were feeling, and in more ways than I could have fathomed. Kelly shared that she had nine losses from pregnancy—some were stillborn and some by early miscarriage. She had six living children—five she gave birth to and one by adoption. We began to look to Kelly not only for knowledge on what steps to take, but also for wisdom on how to handle our emotions.

Whether we realized it or not, this was a small glimpse of God's divine design for our walk. He knew we would need this specific person to guide us through the dark valley we found ourselves in. There could not have been a more perfect person for us to look up to and need during this time of our life. Kelly's level of fervent care set the standard so high in my eyes; this, I am convinced, is how a midwife is supposed to be. Time and again over the next few days and weeks, I would watch her go the extra distance to make sure she met every need she could. I have often wondered how we were so blessed to have her in our presence.

On Thursday, April 16, 2009, my parents' wedding anniversary, we arrived early at Parkland Hospital; I believed I was ready to deliver. Our families took the day off from work and school to be with us through this time. As expected, Kelly met us there. She held our hands as we checked in and were led to triage. Even though some of the staff expected us, most did not, and we had to explain our situation. We stayed in triage for a short time as the nurses gathered our information and developed a game plan for delivery.

They checked on our baby with yet another sonogram. Bobby and I held our breath and each other as our baby appeared onscreen. We were silently praying for the miracle of a beating heart. Again, this was not to be. My heart sank, but we were able to keep our composure. Once the hospital confirmed I was carrying a still child, the care workers were in agreement to induce labor. Our baby boy was head down, which would help us take a go at delivering naturally.

They checked to see if my body was ready for labor. They found that . . . it was not. They explained I would not be having my baby that day because my body needed the day to prepare.

I was a little bummed at the news of waiting yet another day. Despite the fact I was carrying a deceased baby with a frail body that was already showing signs of decline, I still eagerly anticipated seeing the boy Bobby and I created together. Who would he resemble? What would a child of ours look like with our genes mixed together? I hoped he looked like Bobby; I just adored his baby pictures. Would there be any distinction in look, or would he look just like another baby? I longed to hold him and snuggle with his small body.

After triage, they wheeled me to another floor. The staff believed they were helping my emotions by keeping me from other pregnant mothers since my body was not technically in labor. They found available space on the oncology floor and parked me in a room shared with another patient. The hospital rules for this space said I was only allowed one visitor at a time. Since our families could not be with us, they found an empty room down the hall and waited together there. They would take turns spending time with me.

Kelly came in to check on me and give me some things she had brought with her. She handed me a box. It was silky white with two slots for pictures and a ribbon that looped around a silver button to keep it closed. It was a keepsake box. Inside was a preemie-size, footed, one-piece outfit with little lions, crocodiles, tigers, and rhinos. She washed it a couple times to shrink it, she told us, though she had a feeling it might still be too big. Kelly explained that we may want to clothe our baby in something other than hospital attire. She was right; this was something we had not prepared for. We did not have time to go buy something; all I had brought for him was a hand-me-down baby cap from the family I worked for. I knew it might be big, but I still wanted something for our little boy. When I pulled out the outfit in Kelly's box, my heart was warmed. My child was to wear this precious piece of clothing. Perfect for snuggling. Kelly knew just what my mommy-heart needed. She also included a couple of poems one of her daughters, Haley, had written as a means of coping with babies they had lost in her family. They had brought her comfort; Kelly thought we might find solace in them as well.

After some time of being separated from my family, Bobby convinced me to sit with our loved ones in the empty hospital room where they had gathered. It was only two doors down from my room. We were not sure why the staff insisted on keeping me separated. We understood their policy, though I did not belong on that floor to begin with. I was a grieving mother and did better surrounded by people I knew and loved. At first the nurses did not want me to leave my room, but once I explained to them our point of view, they considered my overall emotional well-being and allowed me to wait the rest of the day in the other room. Someone in my family was smart enough to bring cards, so a few of us, including myself, played as the day went on.

Every so often the nurses would check my vitals. A few times throughout the day they would check the status of my body to determine if what they had given me was working, or if I needed other medications to get my body adjusted for labor. By that night they determined my body was ready. They wheeled me to the L&D unit. Next to the door of my new room was a black and white picture of a rose. Being a Rosemary, I smiled at this image. Looking around at the other rooms, I noticed mine was the only one with this special framing. I realized it was the hospital's subtle way of letting staff know the patient in the room is bereaved and that they should govern themselves accordingly. I began to notice that as other doctors and nurses walked by my room, they would rubberneck with a quick view into my room, displaying a somber look. As much as it was not their concern to look in my room, I couldn't blame them. If I were in their shoes, I probably would have the urge to be nosy as well.

Once in my new room, another sonogram was ordered to provide yet another look at our baby, and the same list of questions and information we had given in triage were asked of us once again . . . Something we learned along the way was to just go with the flow when the hospital staff needed information from us. The nurse who asked all the same questions as those in triage somehow grabbed hold of my crushed spirit and made me smile and laugh. She did not crack any jokes intentionally, but she had this marvelous way about her that livened my heart and put my soul at ease. Maybe it was the simple act of continuing to be genuinely bubbly despite the circumstance she was working in. She had dark, smooth skin, a round expressive face, and hair in the form of long thick braids tied down her back. I was drawn to her. I asked if she was going to be my nurse for the night and she replied that she was only there to gather my information. At the end of her questions, I told her how appreciative I was of her presence and that I wished she could stay. My words seemed to catch her off guard a bit as she froze in response, then smiled and said thank you. I remember her leaving the room in a hurry. After the sonogram was finished, she reentered my room with her hands in the air, saying, "Good news! I'm yours for the night!"

That she was! She found a small desk and chair down the hall, brought it to my door and camped just outside my room. She meant it. She wasn't going anywhere and had no other patients to tend to. Whenever I needed anything, she was there to help me: get me ice, find me lip gloss, help me to the bathroom, give me pain meds—you name it, she was there.

Kelly stayed by my side as well. She found a chair and parked it next to my bed. She would pray over me, talk to me, turn down the lights, or just sit there next to me reading a book while I rested.

Eventually, they gave me a drip of Pitocin to help the con- tractions become more effective. I was not prepared for this kind of pain. I don't think any woman is her first time in labor. I fought the contractions, which were extremely painful. Kelly coached me, reminded me to breathe, and put pressure on different areas of my body to relieve the pain. She would have me move in different positions to help make the contractions more productive and make the pain more manageable. But there was only so much movement I was allowed since I was connected to different machines with wires.

Bobby was in the room with us, but he kept falling asleep. Oh, how I wanted to sleep as well. After some time of intense contractions on top of intense contractions, my nurse gave me some medicine that was supposed to help take the edge off the pain. It worked almost immediately, and I found myself starting to doze off. Nearly as quickly as I shut my eyes, I opened them again to the sound of her voice. She let me know that a side effect of this new medicine is for one's oxygen level to lower. I asked, "How do you know if it's dropping?" She answered: "You will want to pass out or fall asleep." Sure enough, that's what was happening. I wanted to sleep, and even I could tell I was going to slip off into a deep sleep if I wasn't stopped. I told her of this feeling and she gave me a mask to administer steady oxygen.

As quickly as I thought the edge of the pain was being relieved, it was back on and now as sharp as ever. I fought the contractions even more. I wondered how someone was supposed to put up with this kind of pain. There was nothing I had ever gone through as painful as this labor.

My nurse checked me to see how far I had progressed. Surely with labor like I was experiencing, I thought, I had to be close. Sadly, I wasn't far from where I started! I was fighting the waves. After a while of sweat and struggle, Kelly leaned over and whispered, "Honey, don't feel like you can't get an epidural. You don't have to do this if you don't want to." By this point I was worn, and her soft words melted me. I didn't realize it until I heard those words: I had wanted to prove to everyone I was strong and capable of delivering my baby naturally. When Kelly shared those soft thoughts, I realized I didn't have to validate my strength to anyone.

I told Kelly I was ready for an epidural and she let the nurse know. My nurse confirmed this with me and had it ordered. The anesthesiologist was great and the epidural worked just as it was supposed to. Everyone left the room while I was given the epidural to allow me to rest. I was able to fully relax and even take a power nap.

I slept for about thirty to forty-five minutes until I was wakened by the nurse and noticed the sink was left on and water was overflowing to the floor! We began to laugh about what we were seeing. There I was, asleep, with water overflowing the sink onto the floor! Of course, someone quickly turned it off, and while we were still laughing, my water broke. The looks on our faces must have been priceless; I'm sure we froze like deer in headlights. It was time.

My nurse ran from the room to gather everyone who was needed. In came Bobby, Kelly, my nurse, and several other nurses and doctors. Bobby and Kelly stood to my left as a doctor stood at the end of the bed to take charge. She directed me to push as she counted to ten. Another push—and our baby boy was out. My nurse picked him up and set him in my arms and laid a towel over him. Bobby and I stared at him, admiring his smooth skin, his perfect tiny hands and feet. He was precious. Our tears and thoughts were just so deeply mixed. I could not believe this tiny little human had been inside of me. Despite the fact he was not alive, I could not get over the fact Bobby and I had made this baby. He was ours. His lips were so tiny and his nose literally cute as a button. A couple of nurses offered to bring all the bathing supplies to us so we could wash and dress him. We could tell he was so fragile and asked if they could clean him up for us. Without hesitation, the nurses nodded, understanding. I handed him to one of them and they left the room.

In the meantime, I got cleaned up. Bobby helped me brush my hair and I lightly freshened my makeup. I didn't want to put too much work into applying makeup because I knew it may not last long with all the crying. Next, Bobby talked to me about our son's name. He had mentioned changing it once before, after we found our baby had passed, but I did not want to. As I've written, I want things "like so," and when my mind is set on how something should be, I'm usually not open to change. Bobby wanted to reserve the name Bobby Lynn Pope IV for our next son. But he respected my feelings on keeping the name and did not put up much resistance.

While I was in labor I had gotten wind of Bobby's Grandma Pope finding something. She was in the waiting room with the rest of our family, reading her Bible and praying. She prayed about a name, saying, "Lord, I don't know if they are thinking about changing this baby's name, but if so, what could we use?" Then it came to her as she opened her Bible. "Enoch walked with God, then he was no more, because God took him away" (Genesis 5:24). When this verse was shared with me, my heart changed. I was preoccupied with labor and had not had a chance to talk with Bobby about this. When Bobby mentioned changing the name again after our son was born, I smiled. I told him I had heard about his Grandma, and I said, "Absolutely. There is no name more fitting for our boy." Our son's name became Enoch Lynn Pope.

The nurses brought our baby back in the outfit Kelly had brought and the hat I packed. He looked lovable and warm in his sweet outfit. As expected, everything was too big for him. The nurses rolled up his sleeves and layered a plain hospital hat underneath the one I brought. I don't remember much of what these two ladies looked like, or their names, but I do remember their demeanor and how they cared for our son. Not only did they clean him up as carefully as they could, they also took time to take pictures of him. They captured details of his hands and feet. They were able to pick out digital frames of baby blue to surround the pictures and handed the physical copies to me when they delivered him back to us. Their acts of giving more than had been asked of them is something I have always remembered. I still become weak at the knees at the sight of those photographs. They were strangers, just passing through, but felt compelled to give more than what was expected.

Kelly brought her camera and took pictures throughout the day. She also had connected with a nonprofit organization called Now I Lay Me Down To Sleep. This organization consists of volunteer photographers dedicated to assisting parents to provide them with keepsakes of their child. She had been in touch with the organization and kept them up to date on my progress through labor and delivery. When it was time, they sent a photographer to capture a few moments of Bobby and me with our son. He was brief and quiet, respecting our space, our needs. Every photograph we received from him was perfect, capturing the sweetest things, details that took our breath away.

Our family filed in one by one to see our son and hold him. Tears and hugs flooded the room. Just when we thought we had swept the emotions away, they would come blowing back through again. One look, one sigh, one clearing of the throat—and the tears would start streaming again.

After everyone left, it was just Bobby, me, and our son in the room. We decided it would be best to say our goodbyes. His body and skin were so frail; the more we held him, the less he looked like himself. It was a hard pill to swallow, to come to the reality of actually saying goodbye, but we did not want our memories or thoughts of him to be tainted. I held him tight and cried sorrowful tears. Bobby couldn't help but join in this painful sobbing with me. After a few minutes a nurse came in and we wiped our tears away. I touched the details of his face, ran my finger over the palms of his hands, and soaked in the smell of his little body. Bobby followed suit, whispering a prayer. As he handed little Enoch to the nurse, he asked if she had a bag we could seal his clothes in. She found a bag in the room and returned his clothes to us. Our baby's scent had been imprinted on our hearts, and we wanted to preserve his smell as long as we could.

We spent the night back on the oncology floor, in a room to ourselves. We cried ourselves to sleep that night, holding each other in the hospital bed. I know the hospital staff believed they were doing us a favor by keeping Bobby and me away from other mothers and babies, but I found myself wanting to belong . . . Later, however, I came to see that, as much as I wanted to be with the other recovering moms, whoever made that call for us did the right thing. I can only imagine what it would have been like for me to hear other crying babies and not have my own baby to take care of.

Enoch Lynn Pope

Birthplace: Dallas, Texas
Weight: 2 pounds, 9.6 ounces
Length: Approximately 15-17 inches
Date: April 17, 2009
Time: 5:50 A.M.

There was comfort in knowing Enoch had already made it to Heaven, that we didn't have to worry about his well-being. He was, and is, in the ultimate safe place. I knew this, yet when people would try to comfort us—reminding me where he was and that I was still very young and had plenty of opportunities to have another baby—my heart would feel crushed. My face would smile at their thoughts, but I also felt as if what I had experienced, and lost, was being discounted too easily. I knew they were right and they meant well, but as Enoch's mother, I couldn't just dust my hands off and be done with my thoughts of him. Life was not fair; I felt as if my child had been stolen from me.

Oh, how I longed to have him in my arms again.

I recently came across a quote by the great C.S. Lewis from his book *A Grief Observed*. The book is centered on Lewis's thoughts journaled after his wife passed away. Though the book is by a grieving widower, he uses an analogy so fitting to the emotions I experienced as a grieving mother. If only I had found this quote all those years ago. I didn't, but that's OK. I get to share it now. I'm sure there is a mother out there reading this book and looking for anything to grab hold of, something to help them, to relate to. Lewis wrote these moving words.

If a mother is mourning not for what she has lost but for what her dead child has lost, it is a comfort to believe that the child has not lost the end for which it was created. And it is a comfort to believe that she herself, in losing her chief or only natural happiness, has not lost a greater thing, that she may still hope to "glorify God and enjoy Him forever." A comfort to the God-aimed, eternal spirit within her. But not to her motherhood. The specifically maternal happiness must be written off. Never, in any place or time, will she have her son on her knees, or bathe him, or tell him a story, or plan for his future, or see her grand-child.[2]

Six

There's a song called "Held," made popular by Natalie Grant. A line in the song says that Providence taking a child from his praying mother is "appalling." And that is just how I felt.

It *was* appalling. We felt so robbed. The closest thing I can think of is a feeling of being robbed, stripped of the most precious and valuable thing we owned. We were robbed of our child and our parenthood: my motherhood and Bobby's fatherhood. Sure, we were young, had plenty of time to "try again," to have a houseful of kids, but all we knew was this one child. Enoch was in fact ours, but then he wasn't. Just as quickly as the flip of a light switch, he was gone. It was unfair.

Bobby's dad suggested to us that it might be a good idea to hold a memorial service in honor of Enoch's life. He said it may not do much for Bobby and me, as we would inevitably feel his loss regardless, but would more so help the people who loved us most. It would provide a place they could mourn and give closure to our son's life, a way they could connect with our suffering. We felt it was a good idea, so we held the service a few days after delivering him.

We asked Bobby's grandpa, Bobby Sr., if he would say a few words and recite the eulogy. He is a numbers man and enjoys finding ways numbers connect. He shared that the Enoch in the Bible was the seventh from Adam. Our Enoch was his seventh grandchild, and I carried Enoch for seven months. The number seven is the number of completion, and that made him smile. We also watched a slideshow from our day in the hospital with Enoch. Although we had enjoyed these pictures before, we couldn't help but weep at the sight of them. There was something about looking at them in the midst of a crowd that was viewing them for the first time. This was an intimate part of our life that we were opening to others.

I also recited one of the poems Kelly shared with me in the hospital.

Held in Our Hearts
It seems like only yesterday
A little one was on the way.
We waited so expectantly,
Knowing all the joy you'd bring.

We talked of names and where you'd sleep;
How you forever we would keep.
Our hearts so full of love and joy,
We waited for our girl or boy.

On wings of sorrow you were born,
Suddenly from our arms torn;
Born sick, too soon, your life was short;
Nothing like we'd always thought.

And now you live in Heav'n above,
Surrounded by our Father's love.
Singing in the angels' song,
One among the heavenly throng.

Our aching hearts could never heal;
Our aching arms, no child fill;
In our home always a place
For you, the child who our lives graced.

Though our arms won't hold you again,
'Til we meet back home in Heaven,
God's perfect little work of art,
You're always held here in our hearts.

We love you!

Written by Haley Nicole Miller, March 14, 2005

Afterward, my Bobby spoke for a little bit, sharing the salvation message. One of the things we did not want was our son's life to have been for nothing. He meant so much to us, and we wanted his short life to leave a lasting mark on this world. Bobby believed it necessary to share the Good News of Jesus Christ. After all, that was the most important thing to us.

We then had a friend of ours we looked up to come forward and say a few words. A few years before, he and his wife went through four miscarriages before they could hold a child of their own. Since that time, they had a little girl and were expecting another baby, a boy. They knew our sorrow and took us under their wings. In his words, our friend spoke of Psalm 31:7.

I will be glad and rejoice in your love, for you saw my affliction and knew the anguish of my soul (NIV).

He interpreted this verse as David singing about how the Lord saw his anguish and gave the love and support he needed at just the right time. He then opened the mic for anyone to speak and share their sentiments. What I expected to be maybe fifteen minutes of passing the microphone turned into an entire hour of people pouring out their love and grieving with us. This lasted longer than the memorial service itself! Our friends and family seemed to be carrying some of the burden to keep the entire thing from being so heavy for Bobby and me. It was during this time that I began to truly understand and feel God's peace that passes all understanding. I could not explain it, but walking away from Enoch's memorial service that night, I had a sense of peace. Yes, I was still broken, but I was able to lay my head on my pillow that night and truly rest. God saw our affliction and knew the anguish of our souls. He gave us the love and support we needed at just the right time. He had been giving it long before we knew the outcome of our pregnancy.

Our friends and family held us that night. They showed us God's love and, in return, we shared His peace. He is a good God. Our midwife, Kelly, also shared a few words that proved to be true. "We were praying that God would do a miracle, and He would show His power over death," Kelly said. "But God's power over death is not limited to raising someone from the dead. His power over death is evidenced in your peace to everyone."

I didn't fully understand Kelly's words in the moment, but as time passed, I began to realize the deeper meaning. I knew Satan wanted nothing more than to destroy us. That is what he enjoys most. He can—and has, numerous times—use the death of an unborn baby to destroy lives, marriages, families. But we were so wrapped in God's love through other people that we were protected. All we felt was His peace. He showed us His power over death.

In the following months, Bobby and I took time to rest. We were not in a hurry to conceive again. Well, logically, we weren't in a hurry; emotionally, we were ready. We weren't financially ready to conceive the first time, but it happened, and we had started to prepare for a family of three. Now, basically given a second chance, and because we knew we wanted a family, we continued to prepare. We made it our goal to wait six months, until we had Bobby's truck paid off.

During that time, we had plenty of emotional ups and downs. There were good days and bad days. Sometimes, when Bobby would work late, I'd go into Babies R Us, or any local store that sold baby items, and linger. I'd stroll the aisles and look over all the gadgets, bedding, toys, and clothing. One time, my heart was hurting so deeply I caved and bought a Carter's newborn-size bodysuit. It was blue and white striped, trimmed in red, and had a little tugboat named S.S. Cutie; in green and white letters it said, "Tugging on Mommy's heart." I could not contain myself. It was all I could do to keep my tears in. I had to have it. I knew someday I'd have a little boy to wear this little garment.

I checked out and left the store just before I became a blubbering mess. I went home and found this stuffed teddy bear I was given in a bouquet of flowers from the memorial. I slept with this little bear every night. I knew it was juvenile, but I didn't care. I found comfort in it, and I needed my arms full. Once I found the bear, I put the outfit on him, but it looked silly, so I tucked it way. Every so often, I'd pull it out and stare at it, wondering what a full-size newborn baby of ours would look like.

It was something tangible that gave me hope for our future family.

Buddy 2012   *Casey 2017*

Bobby and I belonged to a young adults group at our church. One night the group presented Bobby and me each with a gift. They gave me a small sterling silver charm in the shape of a heart with two tiny baby feet embedded in the middle. It was another way of God affirming His love for me. It was exactly the gift I needed.

One of the mental hurdles I had to deal with was the shape of my body. It was no longer this cute little figure. Everything was bigger, curvier, stretched, and saggy. I didn't feel pretty. And I had nothing to show for the reason my body looked the way it did. Sure, my body would have looked this way if I had given birth to a completely healthy baby. But I could say, "Yeah, I have a mom bod, but who cares?! I just gave birth to *this*. Look how precious!" But that wasn't the case, and this small charm gift helped me fill that need of appearance—at least in my mind.

I found an empty chain in my jewelry box and looped the piece onto it. I wore that charm as a remembrance to myself that Enoch was real and that the people around me cared and loved me. I wore it almost like it was a badge of honor. I wore it everywhere. I thought that if anyone noticed the charm they might realize I had a baby even if they didn't actually see me with one. It was through this necklace I could display what I had gone through and why my body was the way it was. Reading this now . . . I realize it may sound silly to some. But this was a true struggle of what I was dealing with and how my mind worked to "fix" my view of my physical self.

A friend of mine also gave me a necklace. It was a cross with little tiny feet walking across it. On the back it said, "I carried you." It brought tears to my eyes to read those three words. It reminded me of my son. I would alternate wearing the two necklaces; they were both perfect in their own way.

Later, I discovered the cross necklace was a piece inspired by the famous "Footprints" poem. I would share it here, but there's too much debate on who the author is! If you have never closely read this poem, and get a chance to do so, please look it up. It is a touching poem that will give you chills. It is a perfect poem for anyone going through hard times and wondering where God is during their struggles and dark valleys.

Shortly after giving birth to Enoch, Bobby and I made the

decision to move. It was time for our lease to be renewed, and management had decided to increase our rent. We were staying in a one-bedroom apartment, and we knew we would like to start a family. We felt it important to find a bigger place to live, but we still needed to pay about the same amount we had been paying. We found an older apartment complex across town quietly tucked away behind trees that made it feel set back from the road. We were able to move from a one-bedroom, one-bathroom apartment to a two-bedroom, one-and-a-half-bath apartment.

I remember some people asked why we moved. It did not make sense to them. Sure, our rent was going up, and it was still just the two of us, but when weighing the cost of staying versus the cost of moving, the numbers didn't make sense to move. But a move made sense to us. Though we had been at our first apartment for two years, it never felt like home. After everything we had experienced, we believed a change was needed. I've noticed some people, after the loss of a child or a struggle with infertility, go buy a car, get a dog, or do something else that doesn't seem to hold logic to the people around them. Moving to another apartment left some people looking at us a little sideways.

This was a big factor for us: the apartment we moved to did not feel like an apartment. It felt like an actual house and a place we could call home. Its "old" feel and architecture brought us the warmth we needed. And this new place was where the bulk of my memories of mourning and seeking the Lord took place. The other apartment was cold and modern, lacking that hearth-like feel.

I tend to be somewhat of a homebody, and though this move did not fix my broken heart, it did just what I expected it to. It became a place of repose.

Mother's Day was around the corner. I had never been more aware of this special day than I was this particular year. I was, in fact, a mother. I deeply wanted to be acknowledged as such.

Just as I had strolled through baby stores, I found myself frequenting the local Christian bookstore, Mardels. I would stroll through the kids section, gazing at all the shirts, books, movies, and toys. Then I'd make my way to the educational section. I'd admire all the curriculum and tools available for teaching; that section was a favorite. I knew I wanted to home-school my own children someday, and I was already getting practice with teaching the girls I took care of. I looked forward to the day I'd bring my own kids in this store to purchase items for our schooling—even if this seemed like a distant dream. After the school section, I'd walk through the adult literature aisles and park myself in front of the shelves designated for parents. I found myself gravitating toward anything having to do with babies: pregnancy journals, how-to books, baby name books—I wanted all of them. Once I'd spent plenty of time there, I'd walk over to the gifts section. I'd study the Willow Tree statues and read the names under each one. Any statue having to do with babies and children, I wanted. During this season of life, I was frequently surprised with Willow Tree figurines as gifts from some of the closest women in my life, and I have a wonderful collection of them today.

On one of my visits into this store around Mother's Day, I noticed a small devotional book called *Mothers of the Bible*. It is written by two women, Ann Spangler and Jean E. Syswerda. I skimmed the pages and knew I needed this book. It's intended to be a twelve-week study, but I think I flew through it in about twelve days! I could not get enough of the words they shared. Each "week" highlighted one mother, or mothers, in the Bible, told a little about their character, what their sorrows were, and joys, and linked Scriptures and promises throughout the week. It also suggested actions to take to live out the Bible.

It was that handy little book that drew me closer to the Lord and seeking His words. I found myself taking away something from each of these women; I related to them in some way.

I found hope at the end of the retelling of Eve's story.

. . . But her firstborn, Cain, became a murderer, and her second son, Abel, his victim.

As the years passed, sorrow chased sorrow in the heart of the first woman, and the last we see of her we imagine her not as a creature springing fresh from the hand of God, but as a woman in anguish, giving birth to another child. Her skin now stretches like worn canvas across her limbs, her hands claw the stony ground, grasping for something to hold on to, for anything to ease her pain. She can feel the child inside, filling her, his body pressing to a way to escape. The cries of mother and child meet like streams converging. And Seth is born.

Finally, with her child cradled against her breast, relief begins to spread across Eve's face. With rest her hope returns, a smile forms, and then, finally, laughter rushes from her lips. Try as she might, she cannot stifle her joy. For she remembers the Brightness and the Voice and the promise God gave: sooner or later, despite many griefs, her seed would crush the serpent. In the end, the woman would win.[3]

I knew of Eve and her temptation, her first two sons, and

then eventually Seth, but I had never put careful thought to what that must have looked like in her life. Eve got her victory. I held onto her story as an example of someone who was once happy, experienced a series of hardships, and found her joy again. I was bound to experience this type of passion again as well.

The mother I related to most, however, was Hannah. She was me. We shared the same desires and seemed to handle them similarly. But there was one difference: for the most part, I kept my weeping behind closed doors; Hannah was known for her outward display of sorrow.

I would seek refuge in Bobby, as if he could make it all better. He would try, but I could tell he simply was not able to fill the void in my heart. My sadness would almost turn to a nag at times as Bobby would get frustrated at not being able to make me happy. Don't mistake my words. Bobby had his fair time of mourning, and we would indeed mourn together, crying ourselves to sleep or through long car ride discussions. There is something different about a mother versus a father, however. It's instinctual; it's how each person is made. Yes, Enoch became our child at the same time, for we conceived him, but I knew him long before Bobby did. Enoch not only changed me emotionally, he changed me physically. There was no part in my entire being that was the same because of that baby boy. He was always on my mind. Bobby, like many other new fathers, really only knew the *idea* of his unborn child. Fathers can't help not being as attached as mothers. Their attachment doesn't usually come until they meet their child face to face. The pain of Bobby knowing his child wasn't with us anymore was there; he couldn't change that fact. It was hard on him when I'd look for him to fix my broken heart, because it was simply out of his hands.

It was Hannah's story that influenced my heart and showed me where I should seek refuge and direction. My heart needed more than Bobby could provide. In Mothers of the Bible, the authors described Hannah so perfectly, and this helped shape how I handled my grief.

Hannah's pain made her seek help from the only One truly capable of providing it.

If Hannah had never had a child, she would still have gone down in Scripture's narrative as a woman of faith. Hannah is not a woman of faith because she bore a child; she is a woman of faith because she sought God when she was in her deepest distress, because she realized that only he could answer her questions and that only he could provide the consolation and purpose in life she so desperately sought.[4]

I realized I needed to look to God for my needs. He was, and is, the only One capable of handling the amount of care my heart needed. Once I started directing my attention to God in this area of life, I noticed Bobby and I had a better understanding of each other and were able to show each other more grace. I was able to spend time with him doing things he wanted, because I knew my need to grieve was being met by the only One who could meet it. Many nights, Bobby would go to bed before me. He knew I needed this time to myself. Once it was just me, I'd turn on a burned CD of songs that carried me to another place. With just the light of a lamp, I'd open my Bible and read. I'd cry and then pray. This is where my most intimate memories with the Lord reside.

I learned from a pastor what the term "giving it to God" means. He was mainly speaking of sin, but I found it applicable to other areas as well. He stated it this way: rarely can anyone "give something to God" one time and suddenly have that temptation to sin be gone, or that problem immediately fixed. Usually, those things have a tendency to sneak back in and try to take over again. You've got to give it to Him, over and over, the pastor said, as if you are needing to break a habit. So, anytime I felt depressed I would pray, turn my special music on, or read. God was there for me, carrying me, holding me. I began to notice that once I had given God all the heartache I carried in that moment, I felt at peace again.

Bobby and I have had well-meaning people we love very much tell us how strong we were, and they reminded us that God doesn't give a person something that person can't handle. For a long time, we were confused by this because we felt so weak. We weren't strong at all. But it was through our constant "giving it to God" that we realized where our strength was coming from: our one and only Jesus Christ.

Seven

September rolled around, and, as expected, we made the final payment on Bobby's truck. It also marked one year since we'd started this journey. I was counting down the days till this month. It meant we could start trying to conceive again. It had been five months since delivering Enoch, and we were ready.

I reached out to Kelly and the other midwives at the Weatherford birth center to let them know we were looking forward to seeing them soon. We figured that since we got pregnant so easily the first time, surely—and without much effort—we'd be meeting with them in the near future.

That first month rolled around and, after the average twenty-eight days, I took a test that showed a negative. Soon after, my period came. There was a little sting in my emotions as the emptiness suddenly felt a little bigger, but I buried my pity and told myself, "Oh well. There's always next month."

Toward the end of the second month, I decided to take a couple of tests; I was past that twenty-eight-day average.

Again, negative. I had thought that, surely, we had it this month. Reality hit me a little harder this time. Bobby tried cheering me up, but nothing he said made it better. I just wanted to be left alone, to take my frustration out on God, and this ended in another night alone by lamplight with the sound of my songs lulling me to sleep.

The next day I contacted Kelly to let her know what I was experiencing and to ask if there was anything we could do. She introduced me to the fertility method called Natural Family Planning (NFP), also known as the Fertility Awareness Method (FAM). NFP is actually a combination of multiple methods used to determine when a woman is fertile and ovulating. It can be used to prevent pregnancy or to be more productive in trying to conceive. (Trying to conceive, in various methods, is given the abbreviation TTC.)

My mind was blown away by the amount of knowledge Kelly shared with me concerning NFP, and I was surprised I had not heard of this information. She directed me to a website, www.tcoyf.com, which stands for Taking Charge of Your Fertility. That link, and a book Kelly loaned me, gave me all the information I needed. I thought this whole process was so cool, and it opened my eyes to the functions of a woman's body. To learn more about the details of NFP, I recommend studying the website www.tcoyf.com; I am not a medical professional and certainly do not want to, nor can I, give professional advice. I will say this: when God designed the woman's body, He knew what He was doing. In His perfect design and purpose, everything works together.

Over the next couple of months, Kelly recommended I follow all the methods in NFP and chart every detail so we could gain an understanding of how my body was working. After talking with her and developing a plan, my mind was much more at ease that I probably wasn't going to get pregnant for at least a couple of months. It did not mean we weren't going to continue to try. I had been given all the instructions for this "project"; I was not going to let us fail.

As the third month of TTC was winding down, I just knew I had to be pregnant. We did everything exactly by the book—I had a fancy graph to show for it—and everything seemed to work like clockwork. I even started experiencing symptoms that lined up with pregnancy: sleepy, hungry, moody. Fact is, those are also symptoms of a period. I would not give up hope, though.

One of the NFP methods is to check one's basal body temperature. I was instructed to take my temperature every morning before I ate or drank anything or even lifted my head from the pillow. Checking one's temperature like this not only helps detect ovulation, it lets a woman know she could be pregnant. After ovulation, a woman's temperature usually rises, and it's said that if it stays elevated for more than eighteen days, it may be time to take a pregnancy test.

I saw my temperature come back down, and eventually I started my period again. Another gut punch. This time, though, I did not let my emotions get the best of me. Or so I thought. I buried them and continued on with life. I tried not to let myself get so low in my feelings, but what this ended up creating was a dull, lazy attitude. I became tired of tracking my cycle. It had only been one month since beginning the NFP method, but I had put so much effort and all my hopes into this method. When I did not get the results I wanted, I didn't want to bother with it much anymore. After all, conceiving was not supposed to be this much work. And it was not the way, I told myself, God originally intended things.

Since I had become apathetic about keeping track of my

cycle, another month came and went—no surprises. I had picked up on my body's cues concerning my cycle, so we still did everything at the appropriate times, but still, nothing came of it. Kelly encouraged me to keep tracking consistently so she could get a good understanding of what was taking place. She also sent me a supplement called B-Fruitful, meant to provide a natural way to help tweak the body and hormones into balance. I did not completely understand what she meant with this supplement, but I took her recommendation seriously.

Back to the charting I went. As directed, I took notes of all details that month. Bobby and I did everything we were supposed to do. Still, nothing. I did not take the negative news as hard this month, though, since Kelly had given me a little pep talk the month before. I trusted her knowledge to find the bottom line with our apparent infertility so we could fix the problem. Sure enough, when I sent Kelly a record of my recent cycle, she saw indications of my body rhythms not working as they should.

According to www.americanpregnancy.org, from which I gathered this basic information, there are two main parts to a woman's monthly cycle, and they are divided by ovulation. The first part of a cycle starts the first day of your actual period, and it ends at ovulation. This is called the follicular phase, and it can last anywhere from seven to forty days. The second part begins just after ovulation and ends when your period begins. This is called the luteal phase. This is a more precise timeline and usually only lasts twelve to sixteen days. During this time a woman's body produces progesterone, which helps thicken and line the uterus for implantation. A woman's body will continue to produce progesterone for a developing pregnancy until the placenta takes over.[5]

From looking at my cycle record, Kelly could see that my

luteal phase was too short. It was only lasting about ten to eleven days. She told me that I very well could be getting pregnant, but my luteal phase was too short, and this was making my body stop producing the progesterone needed to sustain a pregnancy. She encouraged me to continue taking the B-Fruitful supplement since it had the best combination of herbs she could find. Kelly said that if this did not work after another month or two, she would have me add a progesterone cream to my regimen.

It was Mother's Day weekend, May 2010. Over the last few months, I had worked hard at not letting my emotions get the best of me. I tried not to stress in any area of my life. I continued to take life one day at a time, looking for the positives. I was diligent in taking my recommended supplement. Despite my efforts to be, and remain, happy, I still walked around in grief. It was always there. I could suppress it and find something happy to entertain my thoughts, but then something else would trigger my emotions and send me spiraling. C. S. Lewis in *A Grief Observed* described this so well.

Tonight all the hells of young grief have opened again; the mad words, the bitter resentment, the fluttering in the stomach, the nightmare unreality, the wallowed-in tears. For in grief nothing "stays put." One keeps on emerging from a phase, but it always recurs. Round and round. Everything repeats. Am I going in circles, or dare I hope I am on a spiral?

But if a spiral, am I going up or down it?

How often—will it be for always?—how often will the vast

emptiness astonish me like a complete novelty and make
me say, "I never realized my loss till this moment"? The
same leg is cut off time after time. The first plunge of the
knife into the flesh is felt again and again.

They say, "The coward dies many times"; so does the
beloved.[6]

The Saturday night before Mother's Day, Bobby and I went out with a bunch of friends. When we arrived, I saw only the husband of one of our married friends. I asked where his wife was, and he said she was home with the baby. I asked what he meant; I had not heard the news of the arrival of their child. He told me she delivered a couple of days earlier. I mustered up the best happy face I could and gave him my congratulations.

In all honesty, I was truly glad for them, but somehow the news caught me off guard and caused my heart to shatter into a million pieces all over again. I had several friends deliver babies since Enoch, but none of them tugged at me like this one. Someone could mistake my feeling as jealousy . . . and I don't think they would be entirely wrong, as that may have been what sparked the meltdown. But there was more than just shallow jealousy bothering me. I just wanted so badly to be a mom. Sure, I *was* one, but I wanted my motherhood to feel alive again. I felt so empty. Since Enoch's passing, I had started to observe this about my grieving self: the feeling of being alone even in a roomful of people. It did not matter how many people were there and if I was interacting with them, I could feel completely alone inside. And this particular night was no exception and stands out in my mind as one of the most lonesome times I've ever felt. No one did anything wrong; my feeling was a solitary one, and it felt as if I had lost my son all over again.

It took everything in me that night to keep my composure and remain positive. I did not lash out . . . no, not yet. I remember telling Bobby I'd like to leave. He did not hesitate or try to convince me we needed to stay. He knew it was time to go home, and so we bowed out.

We got in the car and not much was said. We drove in silence for a while. I began to weep, and this turned to sobs. My cries became more intense as I shared with Bobby all of my heart—every ounce I was feeling. He drove with one hand on the wheel and the other touching my arm and then holding my hand. He admitted feeling the same sting of emotion from the news of our friends' baby, and this explained why he was willing to leave so easily. Tears trickled down his face as he listened to me. He didn't try to stop or console me. I was so angry.

Some say to not question God. I've never understood this. For it was in that deepest, darkest moment, when there was nothing else I could do, in which I was hopeless and asked Him, "Why?" Why was my son taken from me? Why did You, God, not stop it? Why did You not raise him from the dead? Why do careless, irresponsible people get to have babies and, when we do everything right, our child gets stolen from us? *Why?* It was these types of "why questions" that allowed me to switch gears and pull up out of that dark valley.

I've said it before and I will say it again here. No, God will not give you difficult trials "because you can handle them." I have found this to *not* be true. It sounds good when someone says this to encourage people to be strong, but it just isn't so.

Unfortunately, there are things in life that are going to happen that we, mere humans, cannot handle alone. God loves us and he wants us to seek Him. He wants us to lean on Him, letting Him carry us through the hard times. He is the creator of the universe; I believe He can handle someone asking Him "Why?" He can! He feels our pain. He knows it well.

> *For God so loved the world that he gave*
> *his one and only Son . . .*

God's own child was brutally beaten for every single one of us. He witnessed His child tortured in one of the most gruesome ways imaginable. He knows the pain of a griever. He also knows what is to come . . . there will be a better day. It may not look the way we think it should look, but if we continue to put our faith, hope, and trust in Him—doing so over and over—He will deliver us. It is because of Him that we become strong.

When Bobby and I got home that night, I was still sobbing. He grabbed me by the hand and took me to our bedroom. He knelt on one knee, pulled me close with one hand around my back and the other on my stomach, and began to pray. As the man and head of our household, he prayed with great authority over my womb and our family. Most of the words he spoke have been lost to me now, but the emotions have never left. I do remember him praying that my womb be opened again and that we conceive that month. By the end of that prayer, my tears were gone and peace flooded our home. I was pulled out of that muddy valley by his single prayer to God. There was nothing else that could have rescued me that night other than my husband taking control of our heartache and giving it directly to God. I went to sleep that night more in love with Bobby than I ever have been before—and more thankful for a God who loves us with all of our flaws.

We slept well. It was now my second Mother's Day without a child in my arms since I had been given the title "Mommy," but this year seemed different. I had learned to carry myself with my head up, despite my circumstances, and I was still filled with peace from the night before. Our pastor spoke about Hannah, from the Old Testament book of 1 Samuel. I completely connected with his words. It was as if he composed that sermon just for me.

It was now June and the end of my cycle was approaching. I was beginning to have all the symptoms of pregnancy. I didn't know if my mind was playing tricks on me or if I really was carrying another baby. The day passed when I was expected to start my period; nothing came. Bobby and I decided it was time to test again. I suggested Bobby look at the test first so he could be the one to tell me the good news. He did not want to agree to this plan, though, in case the results were negative. I insisted he look first and promised I would not get upset if I didn't like the answer.

I took the test and left it in the bathroom. After waiting a few minutes, Bobby went to look at the test. He carried it with him as he came to the room I was sitting in. It was hard to read his body language; I was searching for clues. I could not figure him out. I felt it probably was a negative and, as much as I did not want to get my hopes up, I was afraid I had done just that. As Bobby came close, he said I probably did not want to see the test. I had an inkling he may have been teasing me, but I wasn't sure. I snatched the test from his grip, flipping it over to read the results.

There it was. The plus sign we had been looking for. We were pregnant again. I looked at him with mouth wide open and then just screamed. He looked at me with watering eyes. He cried; I laughed. We embraced each other with a hug and jumped up and down from excitement. It had been nine months since we started down the journey of intentionally seeking to conceive, and fourteen months since I last carried a baby in my womb. We were going to be parents again!

> *"I prayed for this child, and the Lord has granted me*
> *what I asked of Him. So now I give him to the Lord.*
> *For his whole life he will be given over to the Lord." And he*
> *worshiped the Lord there (1 Samuel 1:27, 28, NIV).*

Eight

For this child we have prayed . . .

We were thrilled to be parents expecting another child. Sure, we had those "what if" thoughts in the back of our minds, but we were told that every pregnancy is different, so we kept those thoughts and questions suppressed. With Enoch, we had all kinds of tests run to find out the cause of his death. We did not find any answers, so all we could do was take it as a fluke. But we were still extremely cautious in our minds.

It's not uncommon to wait until after the first trimester to announce a pregnancy. Especially if the couple expecting has experienced a miscarriage. We had not experienced a miscarriage per se; that is usually a term reserved for early pregnancy loss. Instead, we had suffered the loss of a third trimester baby. We knew we could not wait till we were "in the clear" to announce, so we felt it best to tell our friends and family the good news right away. As expected, everyone was elated and celebrated with us.

There was the pending question of whether we would use a midwife again. Much to the concern of some cautious—or even disapproving—loved ones, we decided to have another go with a midwife. As I've shared, the level of care I received from Kelly was beyond anything I expected. My son would have died either way, whether under a midwife's care or a doctor's. I learned more than I ever thought one could from using a midwife, and if it was still possible to deliver with one, I was going to. I knew this was not a favorite choice with some of those around me, but I knew what I wanted and needed. If there's a will, there's a way.

I reached out to Kelly and told her the good news. She told me her entire family celebrated when she told them. It warmed my heart. I should not have been surprised by her family's excitement since that's how close Kelly and I had become. Still, her sharing this was another way of showing me that this care was like no other. I wanted it.

Unfortunately, however, Kelly had recently moved to West Texas, where she was originally from. She had finished her midwifery training and had plans to start her own practice in that part of the state. We seriously discussed continuing care with her despite the distance—as if I wasn't getting enough raised eyebrows already. It is not uncommon for midwives to have clients who live full-time in other areas—even overseas—and still retain them for their services. I figured if some of those women, who aren't even on the same continent, can fly to America to use a midwife, then it's not a big deal for me to use one several hours away. When it came down to it, though, Kelly and I discussed this and thought it best to not go this route. Women from other countries come here for midwife care because the care they receive here is better than anything they could get in their home country. The truth for me was that, living close to a major city, I could receive first-class care without me having to travel hundreds of miles to meet with Kelly.

Kelly helped me find a midwife at a birth center close to me. I did most of the searching, but she provided her professional opinion of what she would look for if she were in my shoes. I held my breath as I began my search. I didn't think I would find anything different than what I found the first time I searched, with Enoch's pregnancy. Much to my surprise, I found a place much closer to home. It was a new birth center, one with an experienced midwife, Tina. She had practiced for several years, meeting mothers in their homes, but had recently decided it was time to open an actual birth center. The place was a small home that had been renovated to serve as her center. There were two birthing suites, an exam room, waiting room, office, and one bathroom. It wasn't much, but I liked it; it was quaint, homey. I sent Tina an e-mail, explaining I was an expecting mother and wished to request a free consultation. She soon replied and we scheduled an appointment.

At our first visit, I wanted to be completely up front with Tina about what we had gone through. I had collected all the documentation from my first pregnancy and let her study everything. I wanted to make sure she was comfortable and that we were good candidates for an out of hospital birth. She asked to make copies of the documents so she could review them before making a decision. Overall, the appointment went quite well, and Tina was professional and clear on what she had to offer. I was pleased.

After Tina reviewed my records, she told us she felt comfortable working with us, and we began our prenatal care. Everything was moving along smoothly through the first trimester and into the second. Bloodwork and regular perinatal checkups seemed to be smooth sailing. Being my second pregnancy, I knew what to expect and was more aware of my body and how to take extra care of it. Tina also had an in-house sonogram machine. We would use it to peek at our baby and see a beating heart, but that was about it. To us, everything looked normal.

At the beginning of September, Bobby and I heard a knock at the door. The mailman had two packages, both addressed to me. I asked Bobby if he knew what they could be. Neither one of us had ordered anything. As soon as we stepped inside with the packages, I ripped the side of one of them open to find the book *So Long, Insecurity* by Beth Moore. I smiled because I knew who sent it.

It was from Angie Smith, popular Christian author and speaker. If you haven't heard of Angie, she is the wife of Todd Smith, a member of the Christian group Selah. Angie is a mommy to four girls. While she was pregnant with her third child, Audrey, she was given the diagnosis that her daughter would not be compatible with life outside the womb. Given the option to terminate the pregnancy, Angie and Todd decided to carry their daughter as long as they could. Tiny baby Audrey survived a little more than two hours outside Angie's womb.

So, I must take a step back . . . after delivering Enoch, I remember scouring the Internet for stories I could relate to, real-life accounts that would help me cling to hope. I stumbled upon Angie's blog, formerly known as "Bring the Rain." In it, she journaled her season of life with Audrey. I binge-read through every blog post pertaining to her and Audrey. Naturally, I cried. I thought: *I don't know what's worse, getting your child taken out from underneath you like happened with our Enoch, or knowing ahead of time that the child you are carrying will die soon after birth.*

I followed Angie for some time, and I found her funny, uplifting, encouraging, and . . . oh, she enjoys sewing. You should know I'm a little obsessed with sewing as well. I also prayed she would have another opportunity to have her arms full again, and I was elated when Angie announced she was indeed expecting another child.

Around February 2010, Angie held a giveaway on her blog for Moore's new book, *So Long, Insecurity.* I entered, not thinking I would win; Angie has thousands of followers. To my surprise, I was one of four winners! Angie requested my mailing address so she could send the book. I thought winning was neat, but a few months passed and I never received the book. I figured: Oh well, that's OK; she's a busy woman. I continued to keep up with her blog . . . reading about her new pregnancy, moving to another home, and publishing her book, *I Will Carry You.* The book was about her journey with Audrey intertwined with the story of Lazarus in the Bible . . .

So you can imagine the smile that package with Beth Moore's book brought me. Angie had not forgotten! My heart warmed as I picked up the other package, also with great anticipation of what might be inside. I tore the package down the side once again, and there it was: Angie's new book, *I Will*

Carry You. With the book came the packing slip and a little note from Angie apologizing for the delay of the original prize. I couldn't believe it; I actually won something.

I was more tickled by receiving Angie's book, but I chose to keep it on the shelf until after my pregnancy was over. I did not want to let fear and worry overtake me, so I thought it best to wait.

> *Oh, friend. The Lord cares for us, sometimes*
> *before we ever even know we need it.*
>
> — RANDI FANNON[7]

The date was October 9, 2010. Tina hired a sonographer to come to her facility and perform sonograms on expecting mothers. I was at twenty-two weeks, or about five and a half months. I was at the point when most mothers have a big, but routine, sonogram to check every detail of their unborn baby to make sure everything is growing as it should. Bobby wasn't able to make this appointment as he was working to bring in extra money, so I invited my mother to join me for this visit.

I remember the day well. It was a beautiful, sunny, crisp fall Saturday. My favorite time of year. I wore a simple flowing skirt, a plain maternity top, and one of those crochet head-bands with the flower on the side that buttons in the back, and I had a messy bun on top of my head. I felt cute and stylish for my pregnant self.

My mom and I arrived just as another couple was leaving. There were five of us in the room: my mom and me; Tina; her apprentice, Linda; and the sonographer. Tina and Linda stayed just outside the exam room since it wasn't very big. I laid there quietly on the exam table as the sonographer rolled the wand across my round belly. I was calm while staring at the screen; I asked to clarify if I was having a girl. At a previous appointment, we all made our best guess that I was carrying a girl. The sonographer confirmed that I was indeed going to have a girl. I was relieved and happy; I had been planning for a little girl. I had this feeling long before she was conceived—our next child was going to be a girl. Her name was to be Mary Alice Pope. We always said her first and middle names together. She was never just called Mary. Her first and middle names were family names. Mary was derived from my mother-in-law's middle name, Marie, and Alice is my mother's middle name. My name is Rosemary Alice, so the only thing missing from her name was the Rose. I loved her name because it was so much like my own.

As I was basking in the happiness of this confirmation, I noticed the sonographer repeatedly circling my daughter's head and then lowering to her abdomen area. She was trying to measure the circumference of Mary Alice's head, but couldn't. It dawned on me that something wasn't right as I studied the sonographer's extremely focused face. My heart started pounding, and I asked her if everything was all right. She coughed and said, "Yes, everything is fine." She seemed to stall for a moment longer, then left the room, telling me she was going to get Tina. A wave of . . . well, something not quite right came over me.

I looked at mom and whispered, "Something's wrong."

Mom could only ask, "What do you mean?"

"I can just tell. I think it's something with Mary Alice's head."

About that time, all three ladies entered: Tina, Linda, and

the sonographer. They weren't saying anything. The sonographer picked up the wand to show them, and then pointed to the screen.

I asked, "What's going on?"

Tina replied, though kindly, "We are just checking something, sweetie."

I looked over at my mom, who had stood up to get a closer look. We made eye contact. Things weren't looking good. They took a few still-shot pictures, cleaned me up, and asked for my mom and I to wait in the main birthing suite at the back of the building. Another mother had arrived, and it was her turn for a sonogram.

I didn't know what to think. My hands were shaking, I had a lump in my throat to hold back tears, and my mom and I just sat there quietly. Soon, Tina and Linda entered the room and closed the door behind them. Tina laid the photographs in front of all of us.

"Sweetie, there is something wrong," she said. "I can't say what exactly, but you need to get a second opinion."

I could only fumble out four words: "What do you mean?"

"I can't diagnose, as I am not a doctor, but your baby's head is not round." Tina gently displayed a copy of a sonogram showing a baby with a healthy round profile.

"This is what a baby's head is supposed to look like," she said. "Yours doesn't look like this." She then showed me the picture of my child's head.

"Her stomach is also protruding." She displayed another picture.

At this point, the tears I was managing to hold back broke through and began rolling down my face. I couldn't seem to catch my breath. I was still trying to hold back the floodgates.

Tina pushed through the news. "I can't say whether your

baby will be OK or not, as I'm not a doctor and cannot diagnose these types of things," she said. "I won't be able to provide you care through the rest of your pregnancy. You will need to see a doctor and deliver in a hospital. I'm sorry, sweetie."

My mind was at a loss. It did not know which way to turn, what questions to ask. Somehow, I managed, "Who do I use? Where do I go?"

"Let me make some calls and I will get back to you," Tina responded. "I will let you know something soon."

My mom and I left the birth center and headed to her house. I called Bobby and briefly told him what had just unfolded. I asked him to meet me at my parents' house. The tension of fear was thick in the car on the way home. Neither my mom nor I knew what to say. All I wanted was to see Bobby. He was there waiting for me when we arrived. He tried to be lighthearted and tell a joke, but it didn't work. I asked Bobby to go on a walk with me through my parents' cow pasture. My mom went inside.

I needed to be outside. I couldn't breathe very well. I was still trying to hold things in. Once Bobby and I had walked a good distance from my parents' house, I spilled every detail. I wished he had been with me. Bearing that kind of news without him had been awful. Bobby tried to be positive, but I couldn't be. It did not take a medical professional to tell me whether our child was going to be OK. It was obvious she would need a miracle. Bobby stayed strong and hugged me tight. We prayed for peace, guidance, and wisdom. This was beyond anything we had ever imagined.

Since we weren't given much information, we had hope that

perhaps Mary Alice's condition wasn't so bad. That maybe things were fixable. We began to prepare our minds to care for a child with special needs. We knew that, no matter what, we would take care of our daughter.

We prayed for a complete miracle and hoped that when we went in for another sonogram, everything would be fine, that what we had seen that day would somehow just be a mistake.

It took us a few days, but by Tuesday we had an appointment. Unfortunately, we would have to wait another week. I did not like having to wait; every moment of every day felt like an eternity. I wanted to know what was going on inside of me. I could feel my baby move; she was alive.

The ladies at my church were doing a Bible study. It was Beth Moore's study of the book of Esther. That Tuesday night, after I had been told I would need to wait an entire week, we met for a study. When the study group met, we would go over what we had studied in our workbooks and then watch a video of Beth taking us deeper into the study. This particular night, Beth spoke about God's timing. I distinctly remember her saying, "When it's the meantime, it's God's time." What she meant was this: during the "meantime"—or, a waiting game period—don't worry. God is working on something up in the heavens. This particular video message held with me through the next week. It reminded me to continue to give my cares to God.

On Wednesday, October 20, Bobby and I, along with Tina, had our appointment with a perinatologist who would take a closer look at our baby, Mary Alice. Though Tina could not provide care for us, she offered to come with us to all our appointments free of charge and remain with us through delivery as someone to lean on during this time. Without hesitation, we accepted her offer. We needed her, just like we needed Kelly.

Tina met us at the doctor's office. I remember the office being very cold and yet bright with fluorescent lights. After a short wait, we were called back to see the specialist. This doctor was in his fifties, tall, and seemed to have been looking at black and white videos of babies his entire life. Before he started, I spoke up and explained that we had an earlier sonogram and knew some things weren't as they should be. I asked him to be straightforward and tell us exactly what he saw as he studied our baby. I did not want another episode of what happened at the birth center to happen again. I knew I would not be able to handle it. I know it's protocol for sonographers to stay silent during a sonogram, but I wasn't going to have it that way anymore. I was scared. I had already been devastated, and I did not want people walking on eggshells around me.

In all fairness to Tina, she had not dealt with a client in her practice having faced this kind of potentially devastating news. I was the first. After the sonogram appointment with her, we talked about how everything played out. She apologized for how it had been handled and told me that, since then, she put a plan in place for any future similar encounters. Honestly, it wasn't Tina that upset me, it was the sonographer telling me everything was fine when that was far from the truth. I know that lady was trying hard to stick with what she had been taught in school, to not say anything—but it wrecked me. I did not want that to happen to anyone else. Tina agreed; she understood where I was coming from.

The doctor had no problem telling it like it was. He didn't sugarcoat what he was seeing. We would ask questions, and he would answer them as a matter of fact. He did a quick glance across Mary Alice's entire body, then stopped at her stomach. He told us her abdomen had not formed properly. Some of her organs had grown on the outside of her belly. He also thought there may be something wrong with her heart, but it was difficult, he said, to know for sure. As he moved up to Mary Alice's head, he noticed she had a severe cleft lip and palate. Then he studied the top of her head. He told us her skull was not fully formed; this meant her brain was exposed. He thought she may have a chromosome disorder but could not tell from the sonogram alone. At the end of the appointment, he was every bit as straightforward as he had been earlier. He concluded our time together by telling us that our daughter was "not compatible with life outside my womb" and that I was at risk of heart attack or stroke. He recommended I terminate the pregnancy.

I had not thought about aborting my child until that very moment. All along, I figured I'd carry her, but it was in that moment I began to consider another option.

I remember Tina speaking up and asking for a second opinion. The doctor did not mind the request and had his nurse set up an appointment for the following day with an associate of his at another office. Everyone moved quickly around me as appointments were made; an amniocentesis was ordered to check chromosomes.

The floodgates opened as the news was laid before me. The words "not compatible with life outside my womb" rung in my head. A phrase I had only read about before had just been spoken to *me*. It was an extremely difficult thing to hear. I remember Bobby swallowing to keep it together.

We had been slapped in the face with reality. I asked for it, though. I had wanted the doctor to be up front with me, and that he had been.

Nine

We left the specialist that day empty, brokenhearted. More than ever. We called our parents on the way home to tell them the news and then headed home to cry. We just tried to wrap our minds around this diagnosis. I remember laying down and not being able to get comfortable. Not because my body was actually in discomfort—my heart was. I wanted to wake up from this nightmare; it seemed too painful to fathom.

> *No one ever told me that grief felt so like fear. I am not afraid, but the sensation is like being afraid. The same fluttering in the stomach, the same restlessness, the yawning. I keep on swallowing.*
>
> *At other times it feels like being mildly drunk, or concussed. There is a sort of invisible blanket between the world and me.*
>
> —C. S. LEWIS, A GRIEF OBSERVED[8]

That night I experienced both grief and fear. They

intertwined and could not be distinguished. My heart was heavy.

The next day, Thursday, we went for a second opinion. Something about this appointment felt different to me. It wasn't as cold, and though the severity of what we were dealing with was intense, the air felt lighter when we walked in. It took us a little while to be seen, as they had squeezed in an appointment for us at the last minute, but that was OK. We met with the other perinatologist and briefed him on what we knew so far. Once again, we asked him to be extremely up-front with us regarding what he saw. We needed it that way. He did as we requested, but was also extremely graceful in bedside manner. He was kind and tender to our situation, treating us like human beings. Not that the other doctor did not treat us respectfully. But to put it simply, this doctor was somehow different, compassionate.

This second specialist told us almost the exact same thing as the first doctor, but said he thought Mary Alice's heart was fine and her stomach fixable. Her skull could not be fixed, however, and that was the key to her survival outside my womb, he said. I was perfectly capable of carrying her full term, and I was not at any greater of a risk than a woman having a "vanilla," or normal, pregnancy, he said. He said he wasn't at all worried about my health.

He recommended we get an iuMRI (in utero MRI) to get a better idea of what we were dealing with even though it was obvious there was nothing we could do medically to save Mary Alice. He mentioned a possible chromosome disorder as well, but again, he said, he could not tell from the sonogram alone.

The results from the amniocentesis had not yet come back to confirm or not. Both doctors thought Mary Alice might have Trisomy 13 or 18. They both leaned more toward the possibility of Trisomy 13 because of her blatant abnormalities.

Soon after, we got the results back from the amniocentesis. The test concluded that Mary Alice did not have a chromosome disorder.

Our iuMRI was scheduled for Friday, October 29, eight days later, at University of Texas Southwestern Medical Center. I was about twenty-five weeks at this point and growing more and more uncomfortable.

Bobby and I met Tina at the hospital and got checked in. It took quite a while before I could be seen. I did not want to be there.

Finally, they called me back. I walked down a dark hallway and passed a group of medical students chatting in a small observing room to my right. I entered a bright white room where they had me lay on a table and draped a heavy vest over me to protect my body from radiation. They gave me headphones and I laid there as this big white circle surrounded me. I laid there for an hour, thinking I'd fall asleep, but I couldn't . . .

After it was over, I walked out and passed the same group of students. They were now silent and every single one of them seemed to have somber, even ghostly looks on their faces as they turned to look at me as I walked by. I could only assume they had seen pictures of my abnormal daughter inside me.

I was directed to a small personal office of a pediatric neuroradiologist, who had studied the iuMRI results. I sat between Bobby and Tina as we faced the radiologist.

She asked, "Are you aware of the condition of this baby?"

We all shook our heads and Tina answered, "Yes, we are aware. We were advised to get this MRI done so we could possibly find the reason why this baby is like this."

The doctor cleared her throat and nodded. "Do you want to see the images?"

I turned to Bobby and told him, "I don't want to see the pictures."

Responding, he said, "We don't have to. It's OK if I don't see them either."

Tina spoke up. "With your permission, I can stay and review the images with the doctor."

Relief rushed over me, and I said, "Will you, please?" I paused. "And call me to let me know what she says?"

Turning to the doctor, I said, "I'm sorry. I really can't handle it right now. I can't bear to see those pictures."

"That's OK," she replied. "I understand."

Bobby and I left.

I was fine until I passed the students for a third time. When I saw them, it was all I could do to keep from losing it in front of everyone. My heart raced, my palms were sweaty, my skin was blotchy from hives, and I kept trying to swallow the lump in my throat. I was scared.

As we walked through the hospital and outside to the

truck, I became very agitated. I was frustrated and mad as ever. Bobby tried to console me, but it didn't work. It only made things worse. As we were waiting at a crosswalk by the hospital to cross the street to the parking lot, I lost it. All my bottled-up frustration broke forth—and I was like a loose cannon. I did not care if anyone saw me. I know I looked like a crazy person. I screamed and yelled as the floodgates opened and tears poured down. Bobby tried his best to calm me; I know I must have been embarrassing him. All I could think of was to tell him to leave me alone. The world was going on with business as usual, but my world felt like it was crumbling and there was nothing I could do to fix it. It was all out of my control, and I just couldn't take it anymore. I was overwhelmed by grief.

In C. S. Lewis's descriptions of his grief, he shares from the point of view of *after* the fact—after his wife has died. In my case, my child was still alive. I could feel her kicking and moving about inside of me, but "they" told me that's all she would ever be. It was an odd irony: I was mourning her loss before she was gone. It was as if the individual strands of grief and fear were braided together and had become one rope. Lewis wrote:

> And grief still feels like fear. Perhaps, more strictly, like suspense. Or like waiting, just hanging about waiting for something to happen. It gives life a permanently provisional feeling. It doesn't seem worth starting anything. I can't settle down. I yawn, I fidget, I smoke too much. Up till this I always had too little time. Now there is nothing but time. Almost pure time, empty successiveness.
>
> —C. S. Lewis, A Grief Observed[9]

In a short amount of time this small human being, my child, would face her impending death. And it was all up to me.

Since our visits to the specialists, my heart, mind, and soul struggled with the decision to carry Mary Alice. As I wrote earlier, the option to end her life did not cross my mind until it was given to me. Since that time, I had started giving serious thought to this choice. I wanted so badly for this living hell to be over with. I had already lost one child, and it looked as though I was going to lose this one too.

Bobby and I both seriously considered terminating the pregnancy. We sought counsel from our parents. Everyone around us was as sincere as they could be. No one tried to force any beliefs on us. They knew we had been given an extremely hard choice. You could see it in their faces: they did not want us to terminate, but they also expressed their love to us. No matter what, our families were there for us.

Shortly after leaving the iuMRI, we received the call from Tina explaining what the doctor saw. Thankfully, by this point, I had calmed down. The radiologist was unsure how to categorize the diagnosis for Mary Alice's condition. She did notice Mary Alice appeared to have a very short umbilical cord— only about two and a half inches. She concluded that, basically, she thought that was the reason for everything having gone wrong. The doctor also said Mary Alice didn't have a correctly developing brain, and what she did have would not function as normal.

The talk about her brain did not add up for me. Yes, it was physically obvious her brain was not formed right, and yet it still worked. You see, Mary Alice was an active little thing. Like clockwork, I knew when she was awake and when she was sleeping. How could that be possible without brain function?

I thanked Tina for staying back to gather the information to relay to us. We ended the call. The doctors' bottom-line words were these: our child simply was "not compatible with life outside my womb." We had gotten a second opinion, and a third, and all were in agreement. Bobby and I discussed what we should do with our baby now that we had done every test and scan in the book. It wasn't a long talk. In fact, despite the weight of the subject, there wasn't much to talk about. I was worn out, and I think Bobby was too. His last words were simple ones: "You do what you want to do."

It was Friday, and we had already planned to go to Oklahoma for the weekend with Bobby's family. I really did not want to go, but honestly, I didn't think I would be happy anywhere. My mom suggested, however, that it might do me good to get away for the weekend. Before we left, Bobby and I had a couple of last-minute errands to run. We split up to take care of them because we were short on time.

I was alone and headed to my parents' house, praying about what I should do. I needed to make a decision. The drive was beautiful, like it always was on the road to my parents' place. They lived just outside of town where the houses are a little farther apart. I rounded the first curve with their neighbor's horses to my right and the Dallas skyline hangs in the distance. My parents' other neighbor had two ponds with a few trees sprinkled behind them. The setting sun peaked through, bouncing its reflection off the water, its rays bursting across the sky. Acknowledging the God-painted scene around me, peace came over me and a sureness entered my mind. I made my decision in that moment—to carry Mary Alice as long as possible. She was safe inside me. She was a human being and deserved life, but in all honesty, that wasn't my overwhelming reason to continue with the pregnancy.

I wanted my child. I wanted my motherhood. I did not want these things stolen from me again. I prayed for God to heal her body; He was the only one who could. She was beyond repairable for human hands, and she needed a miracle that only He could deliver. My conclusion that day was this: if He was to heal Mary Alice, I needed to allow Him the opportunity to do so. If I went with my *feelings* to terminate the pregnancy, thus ending her life, I would not be giving Him that chance. No. I would carry Mary Alice as long as I could, praying and hoping for God to heal her body. No matter the outcome of her life, I put my trust in God.

I'm reminded of the story of Shadrach, Meshach, and Abednego from the book of Daniel. These three men refused to bow down and worship the king's gods and statue. They were given a second opportunity to do this when the king delivered an ultimatum that they be thrown in a fiery furnace if they didn't do as he said.

> *Shadrach, Meshach, and Abednego replied to the king, "O Nebuchadnezzar, we do not need to defend ourselves*

before you in this matter. If we are thrown into the blazing furnace, the God we serve is able to save us from it, and he will rescue us from your hand, O king. But even if he does not, we want you to know, O king, that we will not serve your gods or worship the image of gold you have set up" (Daniel 3:16-18).

The same God those men put their trust in was the very same God I was trusting as well. The King of Kings, the one true God. The three men were thrown in the fire, but they were not burned . . .

They saw that the fire had not harmed their bodies, nor was a hair of their heads singed; their robes were not scorched, and there was no smell of fire on them.

Then Nebuchadnezzar said, "Praise be to the God of Shadrach, Meshach and Abednego, who has sent his angel and rescued his servants! They trusted in him and defied the king's command and were willing to give up their lives rather than serve or worship any god except their own God (Daniel 3:27, 28).

When I met with Bobby, I told him my decision. He said he felt the same way. We were glad to be in agreement. We were to carry and care for our child as long as possible.

We left for Oklahoma, packed like sardines in his parents' Chevy Dually, with more of us following in another truck. This was a hunting weekend. I was too pregnant to be climbing a tree stand, however, and I didn't really care to hunt, so I stayed back at the cabin to sleep in Saturday morning. That evening I grabbed a chair and sat on the edge of a field to watch for deer.

I wanted to sulk and let out a good cry since I was by myself, but shortly after parking myself in the chair, I was joined by two hunters who were with our group. They had no idea what I was dealing with, as Bobby and I kept our struggle personal, so I pushed down my feelings and welcomed their company.

I had made the decision to carry my child and felt good about it, but I was still scared and wanted to talk about it. I was still so broken. There were always people around, so there were no good opportunities for Bobby and me to have these deep discussions. I was forced to bottle up my thoughts the entire weekend.

Saturday night, after the evening hunt, we loaded up and headed home. Like many times before, Bobby's dad drove while everyone else slept. Most of the time on these drives back home, I would stay awake. This time was no different. Bobby's dad played through a couple of Switchfoot and Tenth Avenue North CDs, drumming the steering wheel, singing till his heart was content. This was the usual drive home from Oklahoma, something I always enjoyed. I stared out the side window, studying the stars, and sang quietly along with him. A tear fell; I could tell the time was drawing near for me to have another breakdown of emotions.

It was near midnight when we arrived at my in-laws' house. Bobby and I decided to crash there for the night. We got settled in their back bedroom, sharing a twin-sized bed. Once it was finally just us and the door closed, I completely lost it. I did not care how loud I was or the words I used; I was so hurt and damaged. The emotional pain was unbearable. I let God know every one of my thoughts. All the *Why?* questions, all the raging, mad statements . . . He heard them all. In fact, the whole house heard them all. I didn't care. These thoughts had crept in and built up all weekend long, and, in my weakness, I let them all out. Bobby held me close that night, just listening. I cried myself to sleep.

I have never been ashamed of that night. God knew it was coming; He expected it. I'm human. I'm not perfect. I need Him. I felt closer to God that night than any time my entire life. My faith had been violated—and it hurt.

I found a kindred spirit in Angie Smith when I read the words from her book, *I Will Carry You.*

> *I embraced something that night that I will never forget, and it has continued to shape my walk with Him. He isn't threatened by my heartbreak and questioning any more than He is threatened by a rainstorm.*
>
> *He knows that rain will fall.*
>
> *He knows that I will fall.*
>
> *. . . I gave my deepest hurt to the Father, who wanted nothing less than every bit of it. . . . I thought about what it must feel like not only to know that one of your children is hurting, but what it would mean to you if she told you herself—if she came to you because she wanted it to be a shared grief.*[10]

Can you imagine someone you love dearly hurting and not telling you about it? They just bottle it in, or you catch wind of it from someone else and find out they didn't tell you because they didn't think you could handle it. This scenario has played out in my life several times, because there are people who look at me as a goody-goody for my Christian ways. Especially someone in sin who doesn't want me to know about it because they're afraid of what I might think of them. When, in truth, if a loved one confided in me about something they were struggling with, I would want nothing more than to be there for them, helping them with their need. With God, it's the same thing. I knew God loved me, and He still does. I confided in Him that night because I needed Him, and I never felt shame for doing so.

The next morning, at church, I went to the altar and just sat there during worship. I had nothing to say to the Lord, so I just sat there, basking in His presence in the midst of the singing around me. It didn't take long until I felt someone's hands touch me in prayer. Soon I was surrounded by several women from my church praying over me. I could hear sniffles from those around me as the weight of my sorrow was being lifted. Those women carried me spiritually in that moment. No one told them the full weight of my burden, but they knew it was heavy, so they did everything in their power to make it lighter.

We got to know Tina well since she was with us at almost every visit, talking about her personal experiences with pregnancies and the births of her children. Between Tina and Kelly, I have learned that, just because a woman is a midwife, this doesn't mean she has had all her babies unmedicated and naturally. These ladies have had remarkable experiences to get them where they are.

Tina even helped Bobby get a job in the oil field. She saw Bobby and I struggle financially in the midst of our pregnancy. She had a connection to the industry and was able to refer Bobby to those people. Bobby and I have always been thankful for Tina speaking up in this area of our life. It was this job that helped our life financially. We would not be where we are today if it weren't for Bobby getting hired on. We are not wealthy by any means, but it was a huge stepping-stone to move us past wondering which bills we were going to pay from week to week. It was this opportunity that gave us a leg up.

Through all the doctor visits to check on Mary Alice, we were searching hard for a doctor to see me through the rest of my pregnancy. Tina was amazing and, like Kelly, she took the reins and found someone for us. We did not ask her to do this; she simply wanted to. Soon after she told me she could no longer see me for prenatal care but asked to accompany me to all my appointments, she explained that a midwife is someone trained to be with an expecting mother through birth and after. Though she could not be with me in the traditional sense, she still wanted to be there for me. What a gift Tina was. She was the one rational person who could be there to advise Bobby and me every step of the way.

Some doctors she contacted did not want to see us because of the severe conditions Mary Alice faced. It took a few weeks, but eventually Tina found a doctor who was willing to see me through my pregnancy. Since Mary Alice was given no chance for survival, we knew we would not need a NICU. The doctor felt good about our delivering at a smaller hospital. It was decided that, when the time came, I would deliver at

Texas Health Presbyterian Hospital in Rockwall. However, the doctor's next available appointment wasn't until December 1, 2010. It was now the beginning of November, so we had nearly an entire month before I could be seen again for prenatal care.

November was actually somewhat relaxed. We didn't have doctor's appointments to attend. We soaked up every moment, enjoying our time with our baby girl. We would laugh and we would cry . . . sometimes at the same time. Our thoughts grew a little deeper as we pondered the frailty of life.

One of the things that baffled me was the MRI specialist telling me that Mary Alice didn't have much of a brain and that what she did have did not work well. I'm sure she was right, but the reality is we witnessed so much life in this unborn child. As mentioned, she had developed a regular sleeping pattern! She hiccupped, and she would press back if Bobby and I pressed on my belly to feel her. If someone wanted to lean in close and talk to her, she would respond by kicking. The beat of music would get her moving as well. Bobby and I would fall asleep with our hands on my stomach, feeling her move around.

I've been pregnant several times as of the writing of this book, and I can truly say the in-womb reactions we received from Mary Alice were not like any of my other children. It was through her that I learned to soak up a pregnancy and connect with my unborn child. But still, it is true when I say: none of the others ever responded the way she did. She was something special.

Mary Alice was so impressionable that Bobby's Aunt Darla even wrote a song about her. Here is a piece from it:

Mary Alice Time
I'd just tap-tap-tap to you
And you'd thump-thump-thump to me
That was our language of love
I would just tap-tap-tap to you
And you'd thump-thump-thump to me
And I'll always treasure our time

Still, there were times I would find myself in tears and wonder if God really loved me. I'd have conversations with God telling Him that if He was really there and truly loved me, I needed Him to show me.

A couple of days after one of those conversations I met for the Beth Moore Bible study on the book of Esther with the ladies of my church. Almost the entire video from that session was about God's love for us. I can't find my notes on what Beth said that night, but her message was felt in my heart. I walked away, once again, with strength to continue. I felt God's love that night and took it as an answer to my prayer.

There came a day when Bobby and I just needed a good old talk—or, rather, Bobby's parents felt we needed it. And we really did. Life was hard and they hurt for us. Bobby's parents have a beautiful home, one with lots of character. They took us into the sitting area of their bedroom so we would not be disturbed. They wanted to express their love to us, one on one. They shared their thoughts and asked how we were doing mentally.

For the most part, we were OK, but we told them our biggest concern. And this may seem adolescent, but our biggest fear was what Mary Alice would look like when she was born. We loved her inside of me, but would our love carry over once she was outside of me and we saw her face to face? We were legitimately afraid . . . would we be able to look at her? We were so scared to look at the MRI pictures; how would we be able to see her in person? We asked our parents, and a couple of close relatives, if they would love on and hold Mary Alice when she was born if we could not mentally get past the way she appeared.

We ended our intimate talk in prayer, with Bobby's dad leading us. This came as no surprise; he knew just what to say and, like any seasoned pastor, spoke tenderly and eloquently. A portion of his prayer:

> *Lord, we know that you can. That's not in question. But our eyes are upon You. And Lord, not only are we asking, but we know that you hear us when we ask. You said, 'Ask and you shall receive.' And Lord, we are asking right now that healing would take place. We put all our eggs in one basket, and that's in Your hands. Lord, whether you choose to heal Mary Alice or you choose to heal us, we know without a shadow of a doubt that healing is going to take place.*

Ten

I never doubted that He is God or that He could heal Mary Alice. I knew that if it was His will, He would heal her. We thanked Him for whatever decision He would make.
—My thoughts as December 1, 2010 approached

December 1, 2010 rolled around; it was finally time to meet my doctor. I was about twenty-nine weeks along. She was amazing and such a bubbly, outgoing woman. Though she was in scrubs, she had a sense of style about her. She was a go-getter who always looked at the positive side of things, but was also real when she needed to be. I loved her!

I expressed my desire for a natural birth, and she said she would do everything in her power to get me this birth. Since the MRI specialist noted that Mary Alice's umbilical cord was only about two and a half inches, and it had been more than a month since that time, my doctor wanted to have another look at her and asked me to see the perinatologist she worked with.

Five days later, we went to see the perinatologist. We received some greatly appreciated news. Mary Alice's conditions looked the same. We also saw her umbilical cord, and there was more to it than originally thought. We couldn't see it all, but what we did see looked about six inches long. Still small, but that length would give us a little more to work with and more hope toward a natural birth. The perinatologist felt confident I could deliver my baby naturally, but recommended I not go past thirty-seven weeks. It looked as though I would deliver in January 2011.

Bobby left on Sunday, December 12 for a week of oil field training in Oklahoma. My next prenatal appointment with my doctor was December 15. Given the verdict and recommendation from the specialist, we probably would have put together a birthing plan during that scheduled visit.

We didn't make it that far, however.

On Monday, December 13, I felt like taking it easy. I was experiencing Braxton Hicks contractions, so my plan was to rest and drink lots of water. Around 4 o'clock, I decided to fold some laundry, and I noticed the contractions began to hurt a little. This concerned me, so I did an online search of the differences between early labor and Braxton Hicks contractions. Some people said they experienced some pain with B-H contractions, so I wrote off what I was feeling to that. I decided to take a nice bath. With Bobby gone, having these types of feelings made me a little nervous. I shared with my mom what I was experiencing. She recommended I call the doctor or Tina for their thoughts.

I decided to call Bobby and express what I was feeling. He told me I should call Tina first because there was a better chance of reaching her since it was evening. Tina and my doctor had become close, so we knew if it was serious enough, we would be able to reach her.

Tina believed this was just Braxton Hicks as well. She assured me I could come by her office in the morning so she could check me to provide some peace of mind. Since she was available the next morning, I decided to take her offer.

On Tuesday morning I drove to Tina's birth center. The sun was shining this cool December morning. As I headed to the center, I cradled my stomach in one hand. I was speaking to my baby girl and praying over her. I played the song "Beautiful," by MercyMe, on repeat. Something was different about this day. I honestly did not know what it held, but I knew things were different, somehow distinct. I met Tina and Linda at Tina's center. When she checked me, her eyes lit up. "Oh my, you're at a 5!" She asked how my night went, and I told her I woke up a few times from the contraction pain and that it never went away. She said, "Girl, that's not Braxton Hicks. You're in labor."

She told me to call Bobby so he could get back to town. I did, and he was quickly on his way back to Texas. In the meantime, she made a few calls to cancel the day's appointments and called my doctor to let her know we'd be seeing her. Thankfully, my doctor was already at the hospital with another mother. I also called my parents and Bobby's to let them know what was going on and that I'd be headed to the hospital soon to deliver Mary Alice.

While I was talking with my mom, I asked her to grab a few things since I only had the clothes on my back. I also asked her to grab my camera. There wasn't any time for someone from Now I Lay Me Down To Sleep to come, but I knew I wanted as many pictures as possible. Tina overheard me and contacted a birth photography friend to come fill this need.

From the birth center, I followed Tina and Linda to the hospital in my truck. I was alone for a few minutes during the drive. I couldn't believe I was actually in labor. All this waiting would be ending soon. The time was here, and I was going to meet this little being. I wasn't necessarily excited or happy about it, but I wasn't scared either. There was a stillness and a calmness I felt. I knew that, no matter what, everything would be OK. I called Bobby again to make sure he had indeed left, which he had.

Tina, Linda, and I arrived at the hospital together. The front desk receptionist almost did not believe me when I told her I was in labor. I was levelheaded and coherent; I was not in agonizing pain, and I was able to keep my focus on those around me. Tina and Linda explained our situation and said my doctor was expecting me. Before long, a room was ready.

There was a familiarity with a picture that hung by the door of my room. A rose. This time, though, the rose was yellow. My eyes caught sight of the image and I smiled. It seemed to be the same type of subtle message as before, one letting hospital staff know the family is bereaved. I liked that this rose was yellow; I've always heard the color yellow makes people happy. Later, when researching the significance of yellow roses, I found this.

Bright, cheerful, and joyful are what come to
mind when thinking of a yellow rose. Yellow roses
create warm feelings and provide happiness.

—WWW.PASSIONGROWERS.COM[11]

I found it ironic that a yellow rose would be next to my door, but something tells me that whoever made this choice knew exactly what they were doing.

I was hooked up quickly to the machines so the nurses could keep track of my vitals. I was asked about fifty questions about my health. Not long after being checked in, my doctor came to see me. She had been delivering a baby via Cesarean section. She noticed a crocheted shawl I was gifted by the hospital (the ladies of a local Methodist Church made it). This led to a couple of nurses bringing more handmade items made by the same group of ladies. Some of the items were pink and purple; the choice between colors was mine to make. I picked a purple crocheted piece that had long sleeves and pants with a ribbon laced up the middle to adjust the size. This was perfect. I did not have anything for Mary Alice, but this wasn't because I was unprepared. I was. I had already picked out a pink and red knit sweater bodysuit that I wanted her to wear during our time with her, but it was a newborn size, and I didn't have it with me. I never figured I would go into preterm labor, and I wasn't prepared to go to the hospital that day. The thoughtful outfit offered to me would do, and the color was perfect. I chose purple because Mary Alice is a daughter of the most high King. She is royalty and deserved the best.

In sifting through my keepsake items from Enoch, I found

an outfit given to us by the hospital where he was delivered. When they gave it to us, Kelly had already given me an outfit, so this one was never used. As I looked it over, I noticed it was handmade by another group of ladies from a Methodist Church. I've never realized this until now, and I know anyone can make and donate items to a maternity ward, but I want to give a nod to the wonderful ladies of the Methodist Church. What a blessing and a beautiful ministry they carry out. It does not go unnoticed. From one seamstress and crocheter to another, thank you. I know the time, dedication, and concentration that goes into creating these pieces, and this makes me cherish them all the more. You truly touched me.

Soon after getting settled in, the sonographer entered to check Mary Alice's position. Good news: she was head down. We then asked if he could see how long her umbilical cord was. Perplexed by our question, he responded, while sliding the wand over my belly, "Oh, it's right here, and goes all the way over here." "So it's longer than six inches?" we asked. "Yes, there's plenty of cord," he answered. Tina, Linda, and I all celebrated, rejoicing with laugher at this good news. Thank you, Jesus! We knew we would be taking a chance of the cord rupturing at only six inches.

Now all that was left was to wait for Bobby to arrive. We didn't want to do anything that would progress labor, and I was fairly comfortable with the level of contractions, so I did not ask for any pain medication. Family and friends began to trickle in my room to check on me and ask if I needed anything.

Around 2 o'clock, Bobby arrived. I was relieved to have him

with me. Once he was in the room, my doctor asked if she could break my water to get things moving. Honestly, I did not care; I gladly let her. She also checked to see how much I was dilated. I was around eight centimeters. After my water broke, the doctor recommended I get a Pitocin drip in an IV. I did not want one because I remembered how strong the pain was with Enoch. Everything was moving along smoothly without it; I did not want to mess anything up. She insisted, though, and I gave in, with one condition: that I be given an epidural. There was no way I was going to feel that kind of pain again. She obliged; we had made a deal.

The epidural was ordered. Once my pain management was in place, the doctor came to check on me again. I remember her sitting on the side of my bed, talking to me about how the sensations would feel different since I was now numb. She told me if I started to feel pressure "down there" to let my nurse know, because that meant it was probably time to push. While she talked, the nurse administered the Pitocin drip.

About a minute after my doctor left the room, while the nurse was still fidgeting with my IV, I realized I needed to use the bathroom. I told my nurse. She questioned me to make sure, and then she left the room. She returned very soon with my doctor, who questioned me on this. It then occurred to me what was going on. It was time. I didn't need to go to the bathroom; I was experiencing the pressure my doctor told me about.

After we lost Enoch, I remember telling people, "I don't know what hurts worse, being able to see and hold your stillborn baby, or not being able to ever see your baby." By the latter, I meant when someone has an early miscarriage. This, however, was way more intense. I could feel Mary Alice all the time, but I was so scared I didn't know if I would be able to look at my own baby girl. Since making the decision to carry her regardless, this was the fear that tormented Bobby and me.

Soon, there was a lot of rushing around making sure everything was in place. The lights were turned down low with just one light on for my doctor. The baby station was also turned on with a soft glowing light and warmer. Tina and Linda stayed with us and stood by the doctor ready to take care of Mary Alice. Bobby was by my head holding a blanket to shield us from seeing our daughter.

After a couple of pushes, our baby girl entered the world. She was carried to the baby station, for Tina and Linda to look over her. Bobby continued to hold the blanket up as the doctor began to clean me up. Mary Alice then let out a squealy little cry. I remember my eyes got big and I turned to Bobby. He let go of the blanket and said, "That's it. I've got to see her." My eyes followed him to where she lay. I could not see, but Bobby, Tina, and Linda were all whispering. I could not make out what they were saying. I sat there a moment as a tear welled in my eye.

Bobby eventually turned around—holding our little bundle. The midwives guided him to a seat by the window to my right. It was all my grown man of a husband could do to keep the tears in. His bottom lip began to quiver like a child's as he held our tiny girl. I asked, "Is she alive?" He just nodded his head. "Yes." I tried to lean over to see her, but couldn't. I began to panic a little and asked my doctor if she could hurry so I could see my little girl. She shook her head and said, "Yes ma'am. Give me one more moment."

Soon she was done, my bed was raised, and the doctor left the room. Bobby brought Mary Alice to me. He set her in my arms and I tucked the blanket around her face. She grabbed my finger and even held onto the pocket of my hospital gown. I looked her over from head to toe, watching her breathe on her own, studying every little thing about her—all her traits and imperfections. She wore a thin pink and blue hospital cap over her head. The only thing exposed was her little mouth, the bottoms of her ears, and thick, fuzzy, yellow hair, hair that reminded me of rabbit fur, which stuck out the back of the cap. She only had one eye, and it appeared to be blind, and she did not have a nose since she had such a prominent cleft lip and palate. She had a big bubble on her stomach that held her organs. She was missing some of her fingers and toes and had little thread-like string around an area of her arms and legs.

Bobby told me she had a seizure at the table and they all thought she was going to pass right then, but then she began breathing on her own. This astonished us because of all the physical flaws that would keep her from living very long outside my womb.

At this point, I began to realize something: all my fears washed away and peace came over me as the love I had for her grew. I couldn't believe it; I had actually given birth to a living, breathing child. I knew we probably wouldn't be together as a physical family outside of that room, but she was here with us. I was amazed.

As imperfect as she was, she was so perfect to me.

I held her for a while and experienced skin to skin contact

with her. She even let a little cry out when we got her naked, but as soon as she was returned to my chest, she nestled in and relaxed. This thought came over me . . . I had never heard a child of mine cry until that day. It made me smile; I was experiencing motherhood. When it was time to do the traditional stamped-feet imprints, her feet were wiped clean and she jerked back as the baby wipe was cold and tickled each foot. It was amazing seeing her react in these ways because of what the radiologist had found on the iuMRI.

We loved seeing her lively little body. She was the cutest little thing, despite everything. We were over the moon in love with her and cherished our fleeting time together. There was no worry of what life would be like without her. We simply had God's peace, a calmness that passes all understanding.

We had many family and friends, who lived close, come see us. More than we would have imagined came. It was such a blessing to have their support. Everyone who wanted to was given the chance to hold Mary Alice and love on her.

After some time, our little family of three got to be alone together, just the three of us. Since it was Christmastime, we decided to play Mary Alice some Christmas music. Just as we were getting my phone ready, a group of carolers came by singing "Joy to the World." I couldn't help but cry as they sang. Who knows what they were thinking as they sang this joyous, upbeat song? I just had tears, and I'm not sure why. I guess it was that, even though we were at peace with our situation, everything was a bit too much at once and my emotions got the best of me.

My mind still goes back to that moment whenever I hear that festive song. I smile and reminisce, thinking about how my life has been blessed since then. I'll sing along, and every time, my eyes will tear up.

Family returned to our room after a short while. Though we loved our time alone with Mary Alice, we wanted everyone to soak up her life with us. I remember my father-in-law, Pops, cradling her and staring at his only grandchild on earth. Mary Alice took a deep breath and something in me knew her time was drawing near. I whispered to Bobby to ask everyone to leave. I felt it needed to be just us with her as she passed to Heaven.

With everyone gone, Bobby sat on the edge of my bed and I handed him our daughter. Call it instinctual, but I knew it was time. I was given the blessing of carrying this child for months, and I wanted Bobby to have the honor of holding her as she left. As Mary Alice was about to go, we prayed, "Jesus, she's all yours." She took her final breath, and I looked at Bobby and said, "She's completely healed now."

It was so peaceful. Silent. We didn't shed any tears. We held her longer, admiring her tiny hands and feet. I remember lying there in bed with Mary Alice's body at rest in my arms. I looked away, rubbing a finger against the palm of her hand. I never want to forget that moment. I wanted to remember what she felt like in my arms and how silky and delicate her hand felt.

To this day, three children later, I still rub the palms of my babies' hands as I nurse my littlest one to sleep. It always takes me back to that time and place.

My parents had gone home for the day, so we called to let

them know Mary Alice had passed. Bobby's parents had gone to dinner, so we told them when they returned. We let them say their goodbyes; they went home soon after. Bobby and I held Mary Alice a little longer, and then we called the nurse to take her. I held her body tight, not wanting to let her go, crying, this time because she was no more.

Mary Alice Pope

Born: December 14, 2010, 3:49 p.m.
Birthplace: Rockwall, Texas
Weight: 3 pounds, 11 ounces
Length: 17.5 inches
Died: December 14, 2010, 8:56 pm

As much as it hurt to not have our child with us for a second time, we were at peace. We knew she belonged in Heaven. She no longer felt any pain or suffered.

Eleven

By the time Mary opened her eyes, the setting sun had turned the city into a golden land. She smiled, wiping the tears from her wrinkled face. How true the angel's words had been. No woman from Eve onward had ever been blessed as she, the mother of the Messiah, had been. Yes, the past was alive inside her, but it was the future that filled her with joy. Soon, she would see her son again, and this time it would be his hands that would wipe away the last of her tears.

—Book: Mothers of the Bible[12]

I'm no Mary, mother of Jesus, but during that month of December I felt a connection with that woman like no other time. To this day, any Christmas song on the radio that talks of the baby Jesus from Mary's point of view leaves me in tears. That month, it was as if I was walking in her shoes. No, the child I was carrying was not the Son of God, but his mother and I shared a common sorrow. We were both carrying children we were likely to one day have to bury.

We held a memorial service for Mary Alice just as we did with Enoch. It was so odd not stressing how things would come together or fall into place. We had already done it once; there was no figuring out how things should be.

I remember my mom bought me pajamas during that time; they had cowgirl boots all over the pants. The top read, "This ain't my first rodeo." She couldn't help but think of me when she saw the set, and we both smiled when she handed me the gift. Without saying a word, we knew what it meant. It was the perfect gift, and though we were going through something tragic, it made both of us smile, even chuckle a little. I still have that set of PJs today, and they look well-loved.

It was nearing Christmas when we held the memorial service. We opened with my sister-in-love, Molly, singing "Breath of Heaven," by Amy Grant. I remember Molly telling me afterward that she had never been so nervous to sing in her life, yet she performed the song beautifully.

The song is beautiful and could easily be the anthem over my pregnancy with Mary Alice. In this one song you can completely imagine what this young mother must have been going through, and it brought me so close to her even though we were born thousands of years apart. We became kindred spirits, and I looked up to her. If she could handle being Jesus' mother, knowing what she knew, I could hang on a little longer and be my daughter's mother. I looked to her story often to remind me to trust and lean on God even though I did not understand.

Bobby's brother, Josh, who is married to Molly, read the eulogy. Then Bobby spoke for a few minutes before handing the microphone to me.

As I've done research for this book, sifting through every memorable thing I've held onto in the past decade, I found the recordings for both memorial services. I spoke at both, but in very different ways. At Enoch's service, I was still feeling the shock of everything and was almost embarrassed to have a stillborn son. When speaking at his service, I only read a poem that had been written by someone else. I didn't have anything else to say, and I really didn't want to look anyone in the eyes. You could hear it in my voice. Though I decided to read the poem, I did not want to be in front of everyone. I did not want to talk about my son and what had happened to me. I carried on this way for months after his loss.

At Mary Alice's memorial, I made notes and spoke from my heart just before we shared a slideshow of our time together. I was proud of my daughter—not that I wasn't proud of my son. But in some way, because we wanted to keep private during my pregnancy with Mary Alice, after delivering her it was all I could do to contain myself. I wanted the whole world to know about her! At her service, I shared her song and what it meant to us: "Beautiful" by MercyMe.

It was a popular song on the radio back then, and every time I heard it, I knew this song was for my daughter. The song was written by the MercyMe band members with their daughters in mind. If you listen to lead singer Bart Millard describe the meaning behind the song on YouTube, you will hear him explain that the song is about self-worth and the love of God. All those things are true, but my mind depicted it in another way.

The doctors had told us over and over that Mary Alice was "incompatible with life." Medically, there was nothing they could do, so it was as if we were told she was "not worth anything." This news made me struggle for a few weeks regarding our decision to carry her, and then we were frightened about what she would look like when she was born. If her unborn self could comprehend the thoughts we expressed during that time, I can only imagine her "wondering if she ever could be loved."

We got pregnant because we wanted a child to love and raise. She was ours and, despite all her flaws, we still wanted her. We wanted to raise her, or, at the very least, get to see her alive. We wanted her to live, so this part of the song was like an encouragement to her from us. This was us, saying, "Keep going. You've got this, sweet girl. You are worth so much more than what is hurting you tonight."

Every piece of this song reminded me of my daughter. In some ways, it was an encouragement to her, but it also encouraged *me* to keep going for her sake as well. I'm sure the songwriters did not have an unborn child in mind when they wrote "Beautiful," but in all honesty it was perfect for Mary Alice.

Bobby's dad got up and spoke following the slideshow. As with Enoch's service, we had people stand and speak if they wanted. My grandfather, Papa Jim, closed us in prayer.

In retrospect, what a treat it has been to go back and listen to these recordings. Not the parts that have Bobby and me talking—we were a blubbering mess—but listening to the people closest to us speak and share stories. Some of these folks are not with us anymore, and it has been a treat to hear their voices again. These services bonded our family as one large unit, laughing and crying together.

During my stay in the hospital, Bobby's Aunt Darla gave me a Lenny the Lamb Scentsy Buddy. Just like the bear I was given after Enoch's birth, I had something I could hold that represented the child I lost. Unlike Enoch's bear, this stuffed animal has a zipper pouch in the back. The pouch is made to house a scent pack to make the animal smell good. But I saw it as an opportunity for something more.

A day or so after leaving the hospital, I expressed to Bobby what I wanted. I remembered my first midwife, Kelly, relating with me on the loss of her own babies. She told me she would pick up anything she thought might weigh the same as the child she lost—like a tissue box. She would hold it and imagine her child.

With this stuffed animal, its zipper pouch, and Kelly's idea, I told Bobby what would make this perfect. He went out to Dad's barn and found some fishing weights. Bobby put them in a little drawstring bag inside the pouch—adding more, or taking a few out, until my little lamb weighed the same as Mary Alice.

After the delivery and memorial, everything seemed to return to normal. Normal . . . like the months that followed Enoch's passing. There was still a gaping hole inside me that I had become used to living with. But there wasn't much mourning, honestly, because I had already done all of that before Mary Alice was gone.

I am reminded of the Bible passage that tells of David fasting for his ill son's life.

> *After Nathan had gone home, the Lord struck the child that Uriah's wife had borne to David, and he became ill. David pleaded with God for the child. He fasted and went into his house and spent the nights lying on the ground. The elders of his household stood beside him to get him up from the ground, but he refused, and he would not eat any food with them.*

> *On the seventh day the child died. David's servants were afraid to tell him that the child was dead, for they thought, "While the child was still living, we spoke to David but he would not listen to us. How can we tell him the child is dead? He may do something desperate."*

> *David noticed that his servants were whispering among themselves, and he realized the child was dead. "Is this child dead?" he asked.*

> *"Yes," they replied, "he is dead."*

> *Then David got up from the ground. After he had washed, put on lotions and changed his clothes, he went into the house of the Lord and worshipped. Then he went to his own house and at his request they served him food and he ate.*

> *His servants asked him, "Why are you acting this way? While the child was alive, you fasted and wept, but now that the child is dead, you get up and eat!"*

He answered, "While the child was still alive, I fasted and wept. I thought, 'Who knows? The Lord may be gracious to me and let the child live.' But now that he is dead, why should I fast? Can I bring him back again? I will go to him, but he will not return to me."

—2 Samuel 12:15-23, NIV

David loved his son, regardless of how he came to be. He was the boy's father. As Beth Moore states so accurately in her book, *A Heart Like His:*

As he grieved the loss, he needed to know he had done everything he could to prevent the child's death. David did not want his child to die because he did not ask God (see James 4:2).[13]

As I carried Mary Alice, I grieved her while she was here. I pleaded to God, prayed, begged, asked him to heal her. When He didn't heal her the way I wanted Him to do, after she was gone, *I got up from the ground*, dusted myself off, and continued on with life. I didn't realize I had done this until several months later. I had never made the connection between this part of my life and David's story.

Don't get me wrong, I still hurt for the loss of another child, but I was used to the same pain from before. I missed my girl's presence. I intentionally took a great deal of time to get to know this little being inside me, aware that she would probably be leaving soon. I'd stare at her pictures often as they helped me remember she was real, but I couldn't remain in the past for too long. I had discovered how fragile life is, that it isn't something to casually let pass by—and that included my own.

The incredibly wise C.S. Lewis explained this with an analogy from his book, *A Grief Observed.*

Getting over it so soon? But the words are ambiguous. To say the patient is getting over it after an operation of appendicitis is one thing; after he's had his leg off it is quite another. After that operation either the wounded stump heals or the man dies. If it heals, the fierce, continuous pain will stop. Presently he'll get back his strength and be able to stump about on his wooden leg. He has "got over it." But he will probably have recurrent pains in the stump all his life, and perhaps pretty bad ones; and he will always be a one-legged man. There will be hardly any moment when he forgets it. . . . His whole way of life will be changed. . . . At present I am learning to get about on crutches. Perhaps I shall presently be given a wooden leg. But I shall never be a biped again.

Still, there's no denying that in some sense I "feel better," and with that comes at once a sort of shame, and a feeling that one is under a sort of obligation to cherish and foment and prolong one's unhappiness. . . .

Therefore we shall still ache. But we are not at all—if we understand ourselves—seeking the aches for their own sake. The less of them the better, so long as the marriage is preserved. And the more joy there can be in the marriage between dead and living, the better.[14]

Mourning was wearing at my soul, and I remembered enjoying life before my pregnancies. I wanted my happiness back.

When it comes to flower arrangements at funerals or memorial services . . . well, they can be overwhelming. Some don't like to receive them, and some just don't know what else to give. The flowers are nice, beautiful to look at for a few days, but after that, you just have to throw them away. After Enoch's memorial, I was given a mixture of both cut flowers and living plants. The days and weeks following his service showed me that I could find a comfort, almost a type of healing or cathartic relief, in taking care of these plants that remained. Some were easier to care for than others, but eventually I couldn't keep them watered, didn't give them enough sunlight, or they were simply seasonal and it was time to throw them out.

When I walked into Mary Alice's service and saw all the bouquets lining the front of the auditorium, I felt a sense of warm delight. I saw these gifts as a physical form of love from people we knew, and they represented carrying us through our difficult time. But they did a second thing as well: they gave me something to take care of.

I think it's human nature to want to take care of something, to be needed. Those plants were given to me and were now in my care. They needed my devotion so they could survive.

And just like before, some were easier to care for than others. There was one that I absolutely enjoyed, and it was such an easy plant to care for: a cactus. It was a "Christmas," or winter, cactus. When I received it, there were these vibrant pink and white flowers blooming all over it. I had never seen anything like this cactus before. That plant was something I took pride in, and I was able to see it bloom for several winters.

I found joy in that simple plant. Today, on the rare occasion I see a Christmas cactus, I smile and think back to that gift and the joy it gave me.

From the time I knew I was pregnant with Enoch, I joined forums on the Baby Center Community website. I initially began by joining groups of expectant mothers, but as time went on I became a member of groups dealing with infant loss and rainbow babies. It had been some time since I had been on there, but one day I was feeling down and just kind of fed up with pregnancy in general. There are women—I was one of them—who longed to be pregnant. It's a feeling of genuinely desiring to grow another human being and not being able to stop thinking about it if you want to.

Here I was, two failed pregnancies later, and things had shifted in my life. I no longer wanted to *be pregnant*. I didn't care if I got pregnant again.

In fact, I hated being pregnant. Don't get me wrong. I wanted kids, I wanted my own newborn baby, I just didn't want to be pregnant. It had been one nightmare after another, and I didn't want to live that again.

I wondered if I was the only one who thought this way. I thought, surely, I couldn't be. I logged on to Baby Center one day and found a forum for mothers who had experienced multiple pregnancy losses. Specifically, late term losses. I asked if anyone else felt the same as me. I wanted to know my thoughts weren't random, that I wasn't alone. It didn't take long before someone responded, agreeing with me. Our pregnancy experiences were too traumatic; we did not want to chance walking that path again.

It comforted me to know I wasn't the only one thinking this way, and since I found someone with the same feelings, I figured it was probably OK, even normal. I didn't feel like I could express my point of view to just anyone. The voices of those who strongly wished to be a mother? I could hear their cries, loud and clear, and rightfully so. Remember Hannah? That kind of longing hurts something fierce.

In bitterness of soul Hannah wept much and prayed to the Lord. . . .

As she kept on praying to the Lord, Eli observed her mouth. Hannah was praying in her heart, and her lips were moving, but her voice was not heard. Eli thought she was drunk and said to her, "How long will you keep on getting drunk? Get rid of your wine."

"Not so, my lord," Hannah replied. "I am a woman who is deeply troubled. I have not been drinking wine or beer; I was pouring out my soul to the Lord. Do not take your servant for a wicked woman; I have been praying here out of my great anguish and grief."

—1 SAMUEL 1:10, 12-14

Those who struggle to get pregnant and those who have been pregnant and experienced loss both want the same thing. It's an overwhelming desire to have a child they can physically hold, love, and raise. I get that, but I also felt guilty for my lack of any real desire to be pregnant. I was searching for acceptance for my view—and I found it.

As the years have gone by and I've met other women who experienced losses similar to mine, I've noticed several of them left speechless, or quick to shoot down any thought of carrying another child. There are lots of women who share these same feelings.

Can we recognize this deceptiveness and seed of fear that comes from Satan? He does not want us to be fruitful and multiply.

During this period of my pregnancy protest, Bobby and I

were approached about a possible adoption. We were all in, ready to do this. I particularly liked the idea. I didn't have to be pregnant to have a child. This baby already existed and was healthy. I didn't have to worry. I would already know what he or she looked like: color of hair, eyes, complexion. I began to imagine life with this child. The little tot as my sidekick, snuggling on the couch watching cartoons, little kid snacks and sippy cups, getting up in the middle of the night with them. Loading them in the car. All the mundane, everyday things of parenting. After about a month, however, we wondered if this adoption was legit: was the single mom going to give up her rights? Would the grandparents let this child be adopted by strangers? It became clear that this opportunity was not going to happen, that this particular child was going to stay with its family after all.

As things moved toward the close of this adoption opportunity, I prayed God would give me peace to let go of this dream. And that I wouldn't mourn the loss of this child.

When we got final word that this adoption was not going to happen, the peace I prayed for came over me. I did not hurt for what could have been. I simply rested in the fact that God knows what He is doing.

Bobby's job in the oil field had him working out of a yard in Alvarado, Texas. He was required to work long hours, so we quickly discovered it would be best for us to move. A couple of months after Mary Alice passed, Bobby and I loaded our belongings on a flatbed trailer and moved about an hour west of our families. We settled in a 1980s-style, single-wide mobile home that no one had lived in for about six months. The rent was cheap, which was the deciding factor for us to move in. The home sat on a one-acre lot in the peaceful community of Coyote Flats, Texas. Bobby's commute was a breeze; his work was just down the road.

I had never lived in a mobile home before. Bobby had lived in a single-wide as a child with his parents and two brothers. I honestly enjoyed living there, and I told Bobby that my only hang-up with living in a mobile home was the concern of fire or tornado. I know either disaster can damage permanent homes as well, but these types of homes are known for going up in flames quickly, and they don't stand a chance in a tornado.

The landlord had just replaced the carpet and, as I said, it was peaceful. With everything Bobby and I had been through, it was almost as though we were starting a new life, starting fresh. I had a relative that lived in the next town over; other than that, we didn't know anyone.

We thoroughly enjoyed our time in that home. We would set up my laptop outside, sit in lawn chairs, and watch movies under the stars. I remember Bobby coming home from work one day. I greeted him in the front yard; I had been planting flowers in the small flower beds. We ended up laying in the grass, watching the sun go down, talking about life, dreaming of our future and what that might look like. Things were just simple, and the move provided a pleasant change of pace.

Bobby worked six days on and three days off. Once, in early April 2011, when his days off landed on the weekend, we went back to visit with our families. Nothing exciting, just being together with everyone. At the end of the day on Sunday, we headed back to our new place in Coyote Flats. Bobby didn't work Monday, so it was around midnight when we left. There were storms across North Texas that night, so we listened to the radio as we drove. The weatherman mentioned the counties north of us and talked of the dangerous storms taking place there. There was nothing pointing in our direction, according to his weathercast.

As we left the main highway, we passed Bobby's work and headed toward our home. Things were quiet; we hadn't seen a drop of rain. It was nearing 1 o'clock in the morning and we were tired, ready to slip under the covers and get in bed. A few minutes had passed since we drove by Bobby's work, and, nearing our road, we noticed all the outside lights on people's homes suddenly go out. Everything went dark, and rain began to beat down on the windows. Though the radio hadn't mentioned our area, Bobby got an uneasy feeling. He made up his mind on the spot, telling me we were going to turn around and head to "the yard" at his work. He knew it would be open and provide a safe place for us to ride out the storm.

No sooner had he finished the sentence when our truck whipped around 180 degrees, in the direction of the oil yard. At first I thought it was Bobby, and I almost voiced my thought that he had turned too fast. Just as quickly, I realized it was not him that had spun us around.

We came to a stop in a ditch on the other side of the road. We could see trees bending back and forth like grass blowing in a breeze. There was loud static noise coming from the radio. Bobby reached for radio and turned it back to the station we had been on.

"*Attention!* If you are between Cleburne and Alvarado you need to be inside and take cover right now!" the weatherman warned.

I sat there stunned, like a deer in the headlights, soaking in what was happening around us. I went back and forth covering my eyes with my hands, as if not looking would make the situation better. I called out to the Lord, repeating the name Jesus over and over. I could not form the words for an actual prayer. All I knew was to cry out to Jesus, relying on Him to get us out of that moment.

Bobby then changed his mind and decided we should get to our home instead. He said, "I want us to get in that old metal railroad cart we use as a storage shed and take cover from the storm there." I agreed this was a good idea. At that point, it seemed anywhere was better than where we were sitting.

Bobby slowly turned our truck around and got us back on the road and then turned us down the road toward our house. I didn't realize how close we were to home since it was so dark and everything was without electricity. We quickly prepared ourselves for the condition our home might be in.

To our surprise, it was still standing. Bobby's focus was on the road in front of us, so he did not see the trailer as he drove down the driveway, and past it, to where the railroad container sat. My eyes were glued to our home so I could spot any damage it may have taken. Which it did. The first thing I noticed was the bay windows on the spare bedroom were shattered. Something caught my eye . . . and I looked up to see our roof flapping in the wind.

I didn't say anything to Bobby; our focus was getting in that old railroad cart. We made it to the cart, Bobby found a couple of lanterns and turned them on, and we got settled. Once we were situated, I asked him if he noticed our house. He had not, he said, so I told him about the roof and windows. In disbelief, he cracked the door to peer out at the house and saw pieces of our roof flapping about in the storm. He closed the door, latched it shut, and turned back toward me. In that moment, Bobby lost his cool; all he could think was that everything we owned was in that home, and he knew it was all ruined. It was like someone had knocked his legs out from under him. Not that we had a lot, but as Bobby saw things in that moment, everything we had worked for was gone.

I had the same realization, but a totally different reaction. This was good; I was able to console Bobby and assure him we were going to be OK. Obviously, I saw the devastation on the outside and had the same thought—everything was gone. My computer, all our pictures, everything—just gone. But it was all OK, I told myself.

Soon after, we could tell the heart of the storm had passed and we were in the clear. I told Bobby it didn't matter if everything we owned was destroyed. I didn't have an ounce of grief about it, and I could not have been more thankful that we were OK. We weren't hurt—didn't even have a scratch—and things could have been much worse. I reminded him that most things were replaceable and we had each other. That helped calm him.

When the storm cleared, we decided to see what was left of our home. As we headed toward it, we could see debris from our house scattered over the hay field across the road, along with our next-door neighbor's silo.

I had the key, so I was the one fumbling to unlock the door. Bobby stood looking at the damage across the field. I opened the door and was completely astonished at what I saw. I turned to get Bobby's attention, saying, "Look!" We both looked more closely and found our home exactly as we left it! Everything was in place, most things untouched. The roof was gone, but the plastic ceiling was intact, keeping almost everything dry. We walked around the home, gathered our most important belongings, and quickly inspected anything that may have been damaged. Mostly, the only damage was to my sewing items in the second bedroom.

We were amazed at what we had experienced. How we thought we had lost every physical belonging we owned, and how normal everything had been just one hour earlier.

The next couple of days were spent getting our bearings, cleaning up the mess, and figuring out what to do next. Though we had only lived in that mobile home for about six weeks, we felt it best to move to another home, one we found in the next town over, in Cleburne.

After two failed pregnancies, an adoption fall-through, and the threat of losing literally every physical thing we owned, we didn't know what to do next. But we found ourselves in a place of rest, learning to enjoy the small things. All we had was each other, and we were always together during our free time. We'd go fishing, drive country roads, go to the movies, eat out a lot, and binge-watch TV shows rented from the video store.

As has always been my nature, I continued to look to songs that spoke to me of the season I was in. There was a popular song on the radio at the time, "What Faith Can Do," by Kutless. It's an upbeat song that totally captured my heart, and I found myself clinging to the words as hope for what God had for our future. We wanted something more from life, and honestly, we were tired from the past couple of years. We were ready for a change.

The title of the song pretty much sums up its meaning. I like to go deeper when I find a song I love, checking out things like how or why it was written. I took to YouTube for research. I found a video of Jon Micah Sumrall, Kutless's lead singer, sharing that the band paired up with a group of guys who wrote it, and explaining what the song meant to him.

His words resonated deeply. I was tired of Bobby and I trying so hard to have children. Clearly, it wasn't in our hands. I still didn't want to be pregnant. But in Sumerall's words I felt God saying this: "Just trust Me. Try once more."

> *If we hold on to our faith, if we put our faith in God and trust in Him, He will do so much more than we could have ever asked, than we could have ever thought, than we could ever dream. . . . If we have faith the size of a mustard seed, then we can move a mountain. It's not so much about us having tons of faith, but how powerful God is. Hold onto your faith when times are tough, when life is crazy; hold onto your faith and watch what God will do. It will amaze you, it will blow you away. God is amazing.*
>
> —JON MICAH SUMERALL, KUTLESS[15]

Twelve

*Now faith is being sure of what we hope for and certain of
what we do not see.*

—Hebrews 11:1

As you know, we named our son Enoch after the Enoch in the
Bible (Genesis 5:24). The only other place our child's name-
sake is mentioned is in the book of Hebrews. We clung to the
Scriptures naming him. One, because of the obvious connection, but also because of the hope and faith those Scriptures
spoke about. After everything we had been through, we
wanted that same childlike faith. We wanted all that God had
to offer.

> *By faith Enoch was taken from this life, so that he did not
> experience death; he could not be found, because God had
> taken him away. For before he was taken, he was com-
> mended as one who pleased God. And without faith it is
> impossible to please God, because anyone who comes to*

him must believe that he exists and that he rewards those
who earnestly seek him.
—HEBREWS 11:5, 6

As much as I was not thrilled with the thought of being pregnant again, I knew it was time I acted on what I preached about: giving it all to God. I could pray all day long, but there came a time I needed to fully surrender my control and give our future children—literally—to Him. Once I had this revelation, we stopped all forms of contraception, stopped tracking my cycle . . . 100 percent, completely, I gave it to God. Did I like this? Not at all. But I knew it was what I needed to do.

In the months leading to this significant moment, Bobby and I had testing to see if it was even possible for us to have a completely healthy child. From those tests we received the good news that we could, biologically, have able-bodied children. Praise the Lord!

The geneticist concluded that our two children had separate random happenings that took their lives. Enoch's death was unexplained. Mary Alice's was summed up as Amniotic Band Syndrome. What occurs here is the inner lining of the amniotic sack ruptures. Marry Alice's sack broke just days after conception. Mary Alice became tangled in the bands, and this constricted significant parts of her body from growing properly. Doctors aren't completely sure what causes such a happening, but it is said to be a rare condition that is neither genetic or hereditary.

With the knowledge of our test results, we knew we had nothing to lose.

It was July 4 weekend, Bobby was working, and I spent the weekend with my family. I was nearing the end of my cycle and knew I'd probably be starting my period in the next couple of days. One night, as we were having dinner, I felt a burning sensation in my esophagus. This triggered my memory of previous pregnancies. The only time I experienced reflux was when I was pregnant. I had learned not to get my hopes up, and I wasn't really looking forward to another pregnancy, so I put the feeling out of mind. I told myself: If I haven't started in a few days, I'll test then.

I did fine with this thinking until I came home from the weekend. Bobby was still workings his days on shift. I was alone with my thoughts and decided to go ahead and test. I loaded up on a bundle of dollar store tests and stashed them out of Bobby's sight. It didn't really matter if he knew about the purchases or not; I hid the tests for my own sake. I did not want things to get built up with anticipation in case disappointment would follow. I took a test that first day, and it came back negative.

The next day, I still had symptoms I knew came only when I was pregnant, so I took another test. There was an extremely faint line. Too faint to be positive, the way I saw it, so I waited another day.

The next day: a third test. It was clearly positive. I didn't jump up and down, I didn't cry, I wasn't happy, and I wasn't sad. I lined the three tests in a row and studied how the line gradually appeared over the three days. I nonchalantly logged on to the Baby Center website, plugged in what I figured to be the first day of my last period, and calculated my estimated due date. March 12, 2012. My sister's birthday.

Bobby didn't know what I had been up to that week. I knew I should tell him, but I didn't feel a need to work up a surprise to let him know he would be a father again. A hint of gladness entered my thoughts, and I decided to call him right then and let him know the good news.

I dialed his number not knowing if I would be able to reach him. He answered. I could hear the noise of oil rigs and men talking in the background.

I didn't stall. "Hey, do you have a moment?" I asked.

"Uh, yeah, sure," Bobby said. "What's up?"

"Well, I'm pregnant again." I had a smile as I told him, but I was also trying to hide faint concern.

"That's *awesome*," he responded. Bobby then turned to his coworkers and said, "Hey guys, my wife is pregnant!"

I could hear cheers, laughter, and high fives take over in the background. I should have known better. I smiled bashfully but then laughed along with them. It wasn't the first group I would have told this news, but it's totally how Bobby did things. Regardless of the past, we were having another baby, one that was growing right then, and Bobby was ready to celebrate. We ended the call quickly, telling each other, once again, congratulations on our parenthood. We said "I love you" and ended our call.

That was it. Nothing grand or fancy in the announcement; we were going to be parents again. We called our families that night, as well as my midwife, Tina. All were happy for us. We were as happy as we could be . . . given all that we knew from our previous pregnancies. You could say, however, that there was a hesitation, on the part of nearly everyone, to be joyful. Others may not have expressed this hesitation, but they didn't need to; we all felt it. It was as if we were collectively holding our breath in anticipation, wondering if things would be different this time.

When asked what I was going to do about prenatal care, I said I wasn't sure. I was two terribly failed pregnancies deep, and we had moved across the metroplex from everyone, including my midwife and doctor. I knew my mom wanted me to see a doctor and even made a connection for me with someone close to our new place. I held onto the number, but I wasn't confident in the direction I needed to go.

I still wanted to use Tina. I was farther away from her now, but honestly, that kind of thinking does not intimidate me. She knew my history; every single document was in her hands. She had walked every step with me through my pregnancy with Mary Alice. I knew her, and Linda, her apprentice, on a more intimate level because of that. I trusted their judgments.

On the other hand, we had been through a lot. Most people would have figured the decision to be a no-brainer: it was time to turn to a doctor. Something in me, though, could not pull the mental trigger to make the switch.

I recently read an analogy posted on Facebook, shared by Kristine Tawater of the Dallas Birth Center, and I instantly related to this post. I could never put into words or explain why I wanted things to be different than everyone else around me. I just couldn't do it in a way that made sense to others—until I saw this midwife's words.

If a woman spent 10 months planning her wedding, researching all the vendors and picking out the perfect floral arrangements and the perfect venue and going on an exhaustive search for the . . . THE . . . very right and perfect gown, the one that matched the perfect shade of her roses and lilies, and she went through 46 cake tasters until she found the exact right one, and she hired THE perfect wedding planner and counted down the days until THAT very day when the makeup artist and hair dressers made her feel like the most beautiful princess in the entire world, doting on her and supporting her and fanning away her tummy butterflies, and she stands at the back of that church just waiting for the right moment to make her entrance and, just as the first strains of the wedding march start and the doors are flung open to reveal her drop-dead beauty and, at that VERY moment the fire alarms went off and the sprinklers went off and that church was drenched and all her flowers flooded and her cake ruined and all her guests and her precious groom run out into the parking lot because the church is ruined. . . But the preacher walks out and he gathers everyone and he still performs the ceremony with her tattered hair and running mascara . . . NO ONE in their right mind would tell her she didn't have the right to be devastated and trau-matized over the way her wedding day went because "you still got married" . . . [16]

These are two completely different scenarios, yes, but this is still an analogy that connects for me. I got married in a time when Pinterest and social media were still fairly new. My wedding was thrown together in six weeks, yet it was still awesome. Since then, when I hear young brides talk of their "someday weddings," I think about the emphasis they put on that one day, as if everything has to be the biggest and best for that one day. I think they may be missing the bigger picture. That their wedding day is but one day of their life, and one shouldn't stress because of it. A wedding at the justice of the peace, or in a cow pasture, can be just as lovely as in a cathedral. God is omnipresent. He is not confined to a church building. And, at the end of the ceremony, two people become one regardless of all the fine details.

I have to remember, however, that even though things really are that simple, experiences do matter and can have a lasting impact on someone, whether they be good or bad. A wedding day is important, just like a birthday, and should be planned and celebrated as such.

Kristine went on to write:

Then don't you DARE tell a woman she doesn't have the right to grieve a terrible loss of her dreams when her carefully researched, hand-picked, and chosen birth plan goes to ashes and dust for whatever reason because she still "has a healthy baby."

EXPERIENCES MATTER. You can still love a baby and grieve the loss of your plan. This is a truth that needs to be understood. No one ever has the right to tell her to "get over it" or judge her for her choices[;] you know what you do? You listen to her, you wipe her tears, and you help her organize that grief into something she can manage WHILE loving her perfect and healthy baby . . . [17]

Experiencing the losses of my first two children taught me that I can plan all I want, but I need to be OK if things play out differently. Because, physically, it really is that simple—as long as mother and baby are healthy. At this point in my journey to motherhood I would have been happy as long as my baby and I were well, but I knew I would still feel like something was missing if things didn't go as I had dreamed. There was a stirring inside of me.

With each of the first two deliveries, we carefully thought of my future pregnancies and took the necessary steps to preserve my womb.

With Enoch, of all the hospitals in the DFW area, we explicitly chose Parkland. When telling people I delivered there, many nearly cringe because, being a state hospital, it's usually not the first choice of most. I then do my smile and nod to ease them into my explanation of why we chose to deliver there. Because it is a state-funded hospital, we saw it as a place they were the *least* likely to do a Cesarean section. It's a lot cheaper for a mother to deliver her baby naturally than it is for a baby to be born via C-section. If the state can avoid paying for a surgery, it usually will.

With Mary Alice, we found a doctor who was willing to let me deliver vaginally even though her umbilical cord appeared exceptionally short. As you now know, the cord was long enough for a natural delivery.

Neither child was born naturally by chance. In the wrong hands, I could have easily been convinced I was a candidate for Cesarean deliveries, but we fought hard for my body and future pregnancies.

With that said, if it had been clear I needed a C-section for either baby, I would have been fine with that. As I wrote earlier, it really is that simple—as long as mother and baby are healthy. If there had been a chance to save Enoch's life via Cesarean delivery, by all means, I would have been the first to say, "Cut me open."

Please do not mistake my words. I am not against Cesarean sections. There is a time and place for these deliveries. They can be life-saving, and it does not make a woman any less of a mother if this is how her child enters the world.

I'm not saying that if you use a doctor you will certainly

have a Cesarean delivery. I had two babies delivered by doctors, both times naturally. If you look at birth statistics in the United States, you see that the C-section rate is fairly high. With the advances in modern medicine, it's safe to say that some—not all—doctors have delivered babies via surgery out of convenience. I did not want that to happen to me. I did not want to start fresh with someone who did not know anything about me. All this made it legitimately hard to decide the best path for me and our third baby.

Deep down, I knew what I wanted. I longed to experience an unmedicated, out-of-hospital, natural delivery. As I mentioned earlier, I lived relatively far from everything I knew. Again, that didn't scare me, but I'd be lying if I said the opinions of others did not influence me. People who loved me wanted the best for me. It's just that our perceptions of "best" were different. I didn't want to disappoint them, but I also had this desire I could not let go.

While all this was going through my mind, Bobby caught wind of an opportunity through his company to travel and work in oil fields around the country instead of remaining local. His pay would significantly increase, which would be nice, but the downside would be how much we would have to be apart from each other. Instead of working six days straight and then off for three, he would be working twenty-eight days in a row and then off for fourteen. For nearly a whole month he would be gone! We thought back to my senior year of high school when he was a freshman in college three hours away. We made it through that time with flying colors, and we knew if we could do it back then, we'd be able to do it again.

Bobby applied for the position and was accepted. It took a good month before the physical transfer took place, however. He was stationed in North Dakota. That first month seemed to last forever. I worked and could only visit family on weekends, so I was by myself most of the time. Bobby was in a brand-new place he'd never been to, hundreds of miles away from home, with men he had never met before.

After that first month we decided to break our lease and move in with my parents on a temporary basis until we could buy a home of our own.

Since we moved into my parents' home, it once again brought us closer to Tina and all the medical professionals I had a relationship with from Mary Alice's pregnancy. The move made this decision an easier one to make. Once we set things in motion to move, I called Tina and let her know my decision. I'd be lying if I said she felt completely on board with it. In fact, she admitted to me several months later that she was scared to take me on, but with the news that there was nothing wrong with my body, she felt comfortable enough to say yes to my request as long as I agreed to see a perinatologist my entire pregnancy.

Once we got settled in a spare room in my parents' home, I had my first appointment with Tina. It was good to see her and Linda again. It was a tender, lovely place, and I felt those same emotions walking into the center again that day. It was my time to be pregnant again, and, as far as we knew, all was right in the world. We filled out paperwork and went through the usual prenatal care steps—peeing in a cup, weighing, checking vitals, bloodwork.

When the time came to talk about payment, Tina and Linda sort of stalled. In the phone calls leading up to this appointment I would ask about payments and insurance and Tina would always beat around the bush, saying she didn't know and would have to get back with me. Well, now it was time to begin some kind of payment, and I needed an answer. I had insurance and was confident we could pay whatever needed; I just needed the numbers. Linda got silent as Tina explained. She told me all she wanted was one dollar for her books, nothing else. Essentially, she wanted to provide service to me for free the entire way—all of my prenatal care, facility, labor, delivery, and postnatal care. I couldn't believe it. All three of us concluded that appointment with tears in our eyes and hugs for each other. I was in awe of the selfless act of kindness Tina had expressed to me once again. She helped Bobby get hired on in the oil field business, which turned our financial life around, came with me to almost every doctor's appointment with Mary Alice free of charge, and now she was offering her services—what she did for a living—to me for one dollar.

While Bobby was away at work, I spent my days searching the market for a home. I would meet with the Realtor and we would travel around town looking at different houses. It was a time in which the economy was down, and there were several foreclosures on the market. I would weed out the poorer-looking houses and find one I was happy with. Bobby trusted my judgment and gave me power of attorney to sign without him present. He would have a say in our offer price, though. Knowing it was a buyer's market, Bobby would start out with a tendency to lowball on the price. Our offers were never accepted. Eventually, we learned most of the houses were owned by the banks, and they didn't care to budge in their price.

It was now December, and it had been a few weeks of us going around and around with the banks on different houses. We had gotten nowhere, and our Realtor and I had seen several homes. She gave us a list of all the homes available in our price range and requested I mark off the homes we did not want based on our criteria.

Bobby was home for his two weeks off, and I was determined to find something we liked and get it under contract. One evening, Bobby and I sat down and looked over the list I had fine-tuned. I showed him some basic three-bedroom, two-bath homes that appealed to us because of their location and the pictures we had available. A couple were quite promising. Then, in another column on my sheet, I had this other house. It was in our qualifying price range but was more than what Bobby initially wanted to pay. It was also nearly twice the size of anything else on our list. This home immediately caught Bobby's attention. We liked it, sure, but were we being ridiculous to even consider buying it? We decided to narrow down our list to our favorites and kept this home in mind, but off to the side.

We showed our parents the modest options we had come to, and then showed them the other home. We asked both sets of parents what they thought about the bigger home, and what they would do if in our shoes. All four parents, without hesitation, said they would buy it. Not only for its size and price, but because of what that house would do for us when the market turned up again, if we decided to sell.

The next day we let our Realtor know the homes we had

decided on, explaining our decisions. She made the appointments; the big home was placed last on our list of houses to visit. Since Bobby's parents are homebuilders, we asked them to come along with us.

We made our way through the first homes, which all seemed exactly alike to us, with nothing particularly sticking out; there was no "this is the one." We turned onto the road with the large house. It sits right where there is a bend in the road, sitting on a slight hill, surrounded by single-story homes. I've never been one to be showy about the material things I have, and this home made me want to crawl into a hole. If we bought it, I'd feel we were doing just that—being showy. The thing was huge, but here we were. It was a legitimate option, and we were here to look at it.

We walked through the home, counting all the rooms and taking in all the space. The home consisted of four bedrooms, three baths, stairs, a formal living/dining area, an office/media room, and a game room. The home was absurd; it wasn't practical for our small family, but the price and opportunity lined up. I asked the Realtor how long it had been on the market and wondered out loud why this home was still available.

She said, "Three days. But it's a short sale."

Intrigued by the term, I asked, "What does 'short sale' mean?"

She chuckled and said, "Well, it doesn't mean what you are probably thinking. It means the bank is selling it short of what is owed on it. By no means does that mean they will close on the home quickly. In fact, it can take months before they actually close on it."

Since we were living with my parents, I knew we could afford to wait out the sale of this home.

"Why does it take so long to close? " Bobby asked. "Wouldn't the bank want its money?"

"I'm not entirely sure," our Realtor answered. "It's just the way these types of sales work."

Bobby and I did not say one way or the other in that moment; this was something we needed to talk about to make sure we were on the same page and making a good decision. But we left the home viewing that day and immediately realized we should make an offer. Naturally, we wanted to see if the bank would come down on the price, but we also decided not to lowball. We didn't want to chance anyone else finding this gem and slipping in an offer before us. It seemed too good to pass up, and, coupled with the fact that we were living with my parents and had flexibility, we knew we could afford to wait on the bank. We decided to meet with our Realtor that night and submit our offer.

In a day or two, we received a counteroffer. The bank agreed to meet us in the middle, between the list price and our original offer. We accepted.

With the understanding that short sale properties can take up to six months—maybe more—to close, and for no real reason, I decided to start praying that we would be able to move in, even if we weren't unpacked yet, at least a short time before our baby was born. Since it was December and I was due in the middle of March, that gave us three months to close.

That meant it would be a real estate miracle if my prayer came true! It was doable, but would still seem quite miraculous.

Thirteen

Over the next few months, we became more and more excited with anticipation of where we were headed in life. It was as if you could see this momentous buildup of all our seeds sown . . . finally ready to harvest. We were also able to often check on our baby growing inside me, found that my body was healthy, and were buying our first home! Though we had much to look forward to, everything almost felt like an illusion. We thought: *Are these things actually real? Will we really have a living baby to love and raise? Will we really have a place to call home and make our own?* We were reaching major life milestones, and with so much that had already happened to us, it was hard to let our guard down. Slowly, as each turning point proved these things were becoming real, we let our walls come down and were able to soak up this season of life.

At our twelve-week appointment the perinatologist told us we were having a boy when our baby flashed his private parts across the screen. It happened so fast, and the doctor could not get our child to open his legs to show us, but he was absolutely certain, he said. Bobby was thrilled, obviously, but I couldn't take the specialist's word for it. Various searches on the web told me it was too early to tell, and deep down I wanted a girl.

I should have known better, though. This doctor saw babies in utero all day, every day; he knew what a private part looked like, even at twelve weeks gestation! A month later, we were back for our routine sonogram. While the sono tech was looking over our baby, we asked what she saw. Without hesitating, she confirmed we were having a boy.

Bobby was over the moon excited, exclaiming, "I knew it!" I half-smiled and smirked at his reaction. I was just happy our child was still showing signs of being healthy. Sure, I wanted a girl, but I think that was mostly because of everything I had been through with Mary Alice.

It didn't take long for me to be just as excited as Bobby about our new boy. We registered for gifts pretty quickly after finding out. Bobby was still in town, so we made a date out of it. The process did not seem overwhelming to me. When I nannied, I had figured out things I liked and didn't like. Plus, I had a mommy-friend accompany me to register when I was pregnant with Enoch.

We had our baby shower in early February 2012 and had a huge turnout. It was a great celebration of family and friends. The decorations were special and well planned. I had never had such a fancy party planned for me, and I loved every bit of it. From that one shower, we were more than prepared to bring a child into the world.

Over the next few days I spent my time setting up a nursery in my sister's old room. You could say I was nesting. That room was spotless, clothes were washed, and everything had its place. Bobby and I finally let our guard down, and one day we cleaned out the clearance clothing racks at Babies R Us. We stocked up on clothes in all different sizes for the next few years. It was so fun seeing Bobby pick out cool athletic-style clothing and then watch him proudly show my mom. He never wanted me to buy clothing before (though I had). It didn't seem practical to him. But now he was gushing over all these tiny articles of clothing.

We prayed over our baby boy often. I would even say daily . . . or to put it more accurately, several times a day. Through our experiences, we had learned we needed to be more specific in our prayers. I wouldn't say we were fearful, but fear did try to sneak in.

I remember being at our twenty-week ultrasound appointment. You know, the one in which they do in-depth scans of your baby's body. We had been to this office several times. In fact, this was the same place I visited near the end of my pregnancy with Mary Alice. They were aware of my history. Tina came with us since this was an important appointment. The sonographer was doing her thing; she focused on our child's every part. After a while, she became silent as she studied his heart. A lump entered my throat and I had flashbacks to my former sonograms. I knew what silence meant. My hands became clammy; I could feel my skin breaking out in hives. My heart raced. I made eye contact with Bobby and Tina as they picked up on the eerie silence as well.

Tina spoke up first. "Is everything OK?"

The sono tech was stoic in her reply. "Yeah, everything's fine." She continued studying.

Bobby chimed in, knowing from experience that this answer wasn't good enough. "Are you sure?"

She seemed a bit annoyed and shot back, "Yes, I wouldn't lie."

It was as if someone popped the lid off a bottle. I burst into tears and whipped my words back at her: "Well, it's happened before!"

Bobby squeezed my hand and brushed my hair back as Tina found a tissue for me to dab my eyes.

In a moment's notice, the sonographer snapped to reality, realizing that her work was more than just a job to us. We were looking to her for peace of mind over our child's life. Though she was doing her job well, checking every detail, we still needed a little more in terms of bedside manners. She apologized and assured us everything was fine. She continued and, the rest of the visit, told us what she was looking at and that everything was appearing as it should. She reminded us that she did not have the final say as she was not the doctor, but she did not see anything that stood out as unordinary.

One by one, as we walked through the gestational ages and appointments, we faced our fears of the past and were able to put them behind us. We prayed multiple times a day. As I've written before, you've got to give "it" to God, over and over again, as you are overcoming something. We did that by praying. Over the past pregnancies, we had learned to fine-tune our prayers and become more specific.

Lord, we pray for a strong, healthy, whole, lively baby and mother. Continue to give us Your peace, Lord. Thank You for another opportunity . . .

It was a simple prayer, nothing long and fancy, but it was precise and got our points across. We've varied it from time to time to meet the changing needs. If you find yourself in need, please don't hesitate to use this one, or create a prayer that suits you! I've learned the power of being specific, and I believe this is a must.

Toward the end of February, at thirty-seven weeks, everything was sailing along wonderfully. No pre-term labor, and I could feel our baby moving just as he should. One afternoon, I was having a normal, mundane day without much to do. Bobby was out of town for work and I was at a point of . . . pretty much just waiting. Waiting to officially buy our house and deliver our baby. As the day went on, I noticed some swelling in my hands and feet. I figured this was normal. I upped my water intake and propped up my feet for a while. This seemed to help some, but I didn't like to sit long because it wasn't comfortable. As I moved around the house I began to see little specks of stars and noticed my hands swelling again.

This immediately concerned me. I tried to keep calm. I thought quickly to where the closest place would be to check my blood pressure: Walmart. There was one about five minutes from my parents' house. I didn't want to worry anyone, so I left by myself. I drove to the store, walked straight to the pharmacy, and sat down at the little blood pressure station. I followed the steps and checked my BP. It was high—significantly high. I knew it was something to be concerned about.

I left the store and pulled over in the movie theatre parking lot behind Walmart and called Tina. I told her my readings; she expressed that I needed to go to the hospital right then because the numbers were too high for her care. She said, "Just come on to Baylor. Linda and I are already here with another mother who is about to have a C-section. We'll meet you here."

Focusing on staying calm, I called Bobby to let him know what was happening. He was several states away, and I had no clue the logistics of how he could get home. He usually traveled in a company plane to work in North Dakota. He was collected as I told him what was going on, but as I was telling him I had a lump well up in my throat from holding back the tears. He could hear it in my voice and he spoke softly, reminding me that everything was going to be OK and he would get home as soon as possible, hoping this would calm me down.

I got back to my parents' house and found my dad working in his office. I knew I was in no condition to make the drive all the way to Dallas, especially in rush-hour traffic. I explained the high blood pressure and told him what Tina said I should do. I asked if he would drive me to the hospital and, without hesitation, he said, "absolutely." I could no longer hold back the tears. I was a little girl once again, asking for her daddy's help. I cried, very emotionally. One of those cries where you are still trying to hold the tears in and you can't seem to catch your breath. I'm sure it didn't help my condition. My dad, a man of few words, walked over to me, put his hands on my shoulder, and rubbed my back. He said plainly, simply, "Keep the faith."

In an instant I could breathe again and was able to think clearly. We made a quick plan. He grabbed a couple things and made sure my youngest sister was ready to go. I went to my room, grabbed a duffel bag, and quickly threw some things together I thought I might need. A couple changes of clothes and things for an overnight stay. I thought to myself: *this is probably it. The hospital is going to induce me to deliver since I'm already at thirty-seven weeks.* I grabbed the tiny blue and white coming-home outfit I bought from Carter's, a couple baby blankets, and my camera.

Once we arrived, I was quickly given a room. They put both myself and the baby on monitors. My mom met us there, coming from her work, as well as Bobby's parents. I was asked all the familiar questions—normal stats, past births, and much more. Tina and Linda came to my room to be with us as the other mom had just delivered and was recovering. Naturally, after the nurses heard of my history, they wanted all the documents. Thankfully, Tina was there, so she was able to quickly make the call and get them faxed over from her center.

We were all positive that this was the day we were going to have a baby. The "doctor in a box," as they called him, had not seen my records yet, but one of the nurses felt confident enough to begin to prepare me to stay because, with a history like mine, along with the high blood pressure, there was no way I was leaving that hospital without delivering my baby. It didn't bother me being told "my plan" was changing. I had already concluded, in my mind, an hour or two earlier, that a hospital birth was how everything would play out. I didn't doubt my dreams or God's plans for this. I just thought: *Oh well, it is what it is.* As I've written, we had learned to grow accustomed to the ebbs and flows of life. Tina reassured me what really mattered: "that mama and baby are healthy." We were all mentally preparing to meet this child.

After things settled following my arrival, our parents decided to grab something to eat in the hospital cafeteria. Tina and Linda went to check on the other mom. I waited, peacefully, in my room. There was no one I needed to entertain or keep company. I was able to relax.

After a time of resting, the doctor came in, introducing himself as Dr. Payne. He apologized for the wait and explained he had been in surgery. I assumed he came in to break the news, officially, that I wasn't going anywhere.

He then asked this question: "Are you planning on having this baby at a birth center?"

Hair stood up on the back of my neck and I took a deep swallow. I was preparing to receive the third-degree, and I timidly replied, "Yes."

He paused a moment, then smiled. "Well, good luck!" he answered. "You are free to go home and have this baby when you are ready."

My eyes grew big. I was, quite honestly, stunned by what I just heard. I questioned him: "Are you for real?"

He explained that he had reviewed my charts and watched my blood pressure come down on its own, and then pointed to the screen. I looked over to see that my BP had returned to normal. He wrapped up by telling me the nurse would be back to dismiss me, and I was good to go. He left, and I never saw that kind doctor again.

Shortly after, Tina and Linda returned. I told them what the doctor said. They couldn't believe it. It was unheard of for a doctor to release a patient so she could have her baby in an out-of-hospital setting. They jumped with excitement when they realized it wasn't a joke. My parents came back in and I told them the news. They were just as surprised.

Tina told me later how much peace she had after my visit in that hospital. Not that she or I needed it, but it was like we had approval in all that mattered. My baby was going to be born—in her care at her birth center.

I didn't have any more blood pressure issues, and Bobby eventually made it home. I had told him he didn't have to come, but he didn't care. His employer was very generous, and he gave Bobby the time to stay with me for the next month. Bobby was adamant. I couldn't blame him. He didn't want to miss anything else and, honestly, I didn't either.

As time drew nearer to our due date, it meant that more time was passing and the window for us to close on our house before this baby was narrowing. We had prayed about being moved in, even if we weren't unpacked, before our child was born, but it didn't look like this was going to happen. There was no talk from the bank, or our Realtor, that this was happening anytime soon. At some point, Bobby prayed more specifically that we would move in on the fifteenth of March. This was after the due date, but for some reason this date stuck in his mind.

On my due date, Monday, March 12, Bobby and I, along with my sister Mackenzie and my dear friend Nyla, went to the park by the house to go walking. Of course, we couldn't go to the park without showing them the house. They were so excited about the home, so we drove them by it before heading to the park. We thought all we would do was look from the road. I was tired and kind of bummed that it didn't look like our hopes and prayers for this house were going to come together in time for our baby boy's arrival. But Mackenzie and Nyla thought differently. They were so happy for us. They wanted to get out, walk around the house, and peek through the windows. I stayed in the truck while Bobby got out with them. As they were walking up, Bobby noticed the front door was cracked open and the doorjamb ruined from someone having broken into the vacant structure. He opened the door to find teenage kids scattering out the back of the house. He told Nyla and Mackenzie to get back in the truck while he went inside to inspect the house. He returned after he found it was cleared; he let us know it was OK to come in. We all stepped out; there was no way I was staying in the truck.

Bobby and I inspected each room while Nyla and Mackenzie self-toured the house. We found writing on the walls, fire burns on the carpet, and evidence of drug use dropped in the backyard. Clearly, this house had become a neighborhood hangout! We figured it was important to let our Realtor know right away. Bobby called and told her as we left the house to go to the park; she then called the listing Realtor. About thirty minutes later we received a very unexpected call from our Realtor. It was pretty obvious that the only reason these kids were in there was because the place was vacant. To keep them from coming back and causing more damage, the seller decided to let us move in—rent free—until we closed.

This was unheard of! I was a Realtor for a while, so I can attest that no Realtor—whether they are representing the seller or buyer—wants the future owner to move into a house before closing . . . and for *free*?! Yeah. That never happens. We immediately knew that our prayer was being answered.

Remember what I said about being specific in your prayers?

We signed the lease agreement that night and spent the next couple of days getting utilities turned on, replacing the doorjamb and lock, cleaning, shampooing carpets. As you might imagine, I mainly just did a lot of supervising.

By Thursday, March 15, we were ready to move in. Close friends and family gathered to help us move. It was exciting witnessing our prayer being fulfilled. Around 9:30 p.m., Bobby and I were alone in the house while everyone else went to get another load of stuff. We sat down and took a break together. We were both exhausted.

While we were sitting there I had a realization that turned into a concern; I shared it with Bobby. So far, our prayers had been answered. I prayed we would move into our house, even if we weren't unpacked, before our baby was born. Bobby prayed more specifically that we would move in on March 15. That was all great, but there was something we did not consider when we made those prayers—we were worn out. I was afraid I was going to go into labor and not have the energy to deliver. Peacefully, Bobby spoke another prayer. He asked that we would get a full night's rest and wake up in labor the next morning.

This gave me a peace, an assurance, that I would have plenty of fuel to take on the next day.

Around 9 o'clock the next morning, I awoke to the sun shining brightly through the windows of my parents' sunroom, where Bobby and I were temporarily living. I felt a tightening around my abdomen and instantly knew it could only mean one thing. I was in labor. It was too early in the day to be Braxton Hicks. I hadn't even rolled out of bed. *This has got to be the real deal,* I told myself. In the stillness of the morning, with Bobby sound asleep next to me, I timed the contractions. After about thirty minutes I concluded they were coming consistently every five minutes. I tiptoed—as one does in labor at forty weeks, four days—to the bathroom to take a shower and get ready for the day. I finished my shower around 10 a.m. and figured I should wake Bobby and tell him about the contractions. I then called Tina and informed her of my status. She was overjoyed and told us both she and Linda would be ready and waiting to meet us whenever I felt like heading to the birth center.

A few moments after we hung up the phone, I received a text from Tina. She wrote: "Do you know what today is?"

I snickered at her question; I had an inkling of what she was thinking. But I replied, "What do you mean?"

She quickly responded: "3:16."

And I tapped: "John."

Smiling ear to ear, I sent a quick prayer up to God, saying, "Of course. This is exactly how You roll."

We were in the middle of unpacking, and I was in labor, but in all honesty, I never felt more like a princess than I did that day. Bobby and I weren't in a rush for anything. We decided to go to our new home and unpack until I felt it was time to head to the birth center instead of waiting around. While unpacking our kitchen, I told Bobby I wanted to straighten my hair. I wanted to look as good as a woman can in labor because we had a birth photographer who would be taking pictures at some point.

Bobby found a chair, brought it to our bathroom, and had me sit down. Strand by strand, he flat-ironed my hair. He took his time, making sure every piece was straight and free of fly-aways. All this while I sat quietly taking on wave after wave of contractions.

It was a moment I cherish in my memory. I was carrying Bobby's child, but I was also the biggest I had ever been. He knew how pregnancy had taken a toll on my body, yet he adored me anyway. It brings an extra sparkle to my eyes to think about his enduring love for me. I may seem sweet and meek, but I don't go without fault. He has seen me at my worst, yet he still chooses me. He is as good looking as any Hemsworth brother, but he still finds me beautiful and worthy after all these years.

A bit later, my mom and Mackenzie came by to help us unpack. When they arrived, I thought it necessary to tell them I was in labor. About two hours later it became hard to remain relaxed through the contractions, and it was a challenge just to think about unpacking. I felt it was time Bobby and I head to the birth center.

My mom and Mackenzie wanted to come with us. I didn't blame them. I would have wanted to as well. But I did not know how I would act in labor. Bobby and I had found ourselves secretive about my labor. We weren't in a hurry to let the news out. With the birth center so small, I didn't want anyone there waiting for me to deliver. I did not want family and friends seeing me in that state, nor did I want to be overwhelmed by a large number of people producing a pressure in me to get my baby out.

We called Tina on the way to the center to let her know we had left. Bobby then called his mom to let her know. When we arrived at the birth center, we were greeted by Tina and Linda. Just by talking and sharing a few things, they could tell my body wasn't ready for pushing. Tina checked my cervix to confirm. I was dilated to about a five. She recommended Bobby and I go to the nearby park and walk to get labor moving. Linda drove us with the anticipation that, by the time we left the park, I would need Bobby focusing on me and not driving.

Turns out, she was right. We had a good stroll around the park, stopping every time I had a contraction. When one would come, Linda instructed me to squat and breathe as they passed.

About thirty minutes into this walk, we could tell it was time to go. The transition phase was approaching, and it was apparent to those around us that I was in active labor. There was no faking normalcy at this point. We were shuffling our way back to the car when I had to stop and endure a contraction. My breathing was deep, and I held onto Bobby's hand for balance. There was a family close by fishing at a pond. Their son looked over at us—he was maybe five or six—pointed, and shouted, "I think that lady is having a baby!" In embarrassment, his parents snatched him around to direct his attention back to the fish. I thought it was funny and I just tried to imagine what could possibly be going through their minds. That family's actions briefly took my mind off what I was feeling, but I soon came back to reality with the intensity of a contraction rounding off.

The short—two minutes!—drive back to the birth center was awful. I felt every bump in the road and could not get comfortable. Contractions were coming one right after the other. I was in transition. Linda kept reminding me to breathe while she maneuvered our way back.

When we arrived, Tina had water running in the tub. She was preparing for me to get in so the painful edge of contractions would lessen. Before I entered, though, she needed to check my cervix. She didn't want me getting in the water too soon because sometimes it can relax a mother too much and stall labor. If someone is far enough along, though, it's usually not a problem to get in the water. It was a huge relief when Tina gave me the go-ahead to get in the water.

I had dreamed of having a water birth. Everyone talked so highly of this kind of delivery. I was looking forward to the warm water. I thought: Isn't this so neat? God provided a natural way to help mothers endure the pain of labor. I eased my way into the water . . . but I soon found myself wanting out. I could not get comfortable at all.

It's said that laboring women will instinctively want to position themselves in different ways depending on how their baby is positioned. I wanted to be on my hands and knees during contractions and still be able to relax between each. Relaxing meant getting off my knees and sitting back. All this was too much movement, though. Tina suggested I get out and try some different positions. We worked our way around the birth room, but nothing seemed to work. I was miserable.

I was questioning myself: *What in the world am I doing? Why did I think this was a good idea? This is awful!* I just wanted it to be over with. And, this: *I'm so tired!*

I thought that, literally, I was going to be in this intense labor the rest of my life! I could see no end in sight.

I could only voice this to Tina: "I'm so tired. I just want to go to sleep. I can't do this."

"Sweetie, you are so far along," Tina told me. "If we take you to a hospital, there is nothing they can do but let you labor."

With that response in mind, I took to prayer. To myself, I

prayed, "Jesus, help me. I cannot do this alone." Immediately, I felt determination, and I was suddenly empowered to deliver my baby.

Throughout labor, Tina and Linda intermittently listened for my baby's heartbeat. Then it was time for another check with the doppler. When they put the wand on my stomach, I was in the middle of a contraction. I could hear his heartbeat, and it was significantly lower.

For a moment, I thought this: *I guess I won't be bringing another child home. I'm losing another baby.* Then I heard a still, small voice say, "Trust these midwives. They know what they are doing."

I caught Tina and Linda in my peripheral, glancing at each other. Tina quickly said, "OK, Rosie, we need you to get up. We've got to get you in another position." She paused a moment, then went on. "Let's get you over to the bed and get you back on your hands and knees. We are going to put a stack of pillows underneath you so you can still rest in between contractions." I was game, ready to move, despite the contraction I was dealing with at that moment.

In very little time I was settled on the bed in my ideal position. From that point on, I could not have had a better setup. Once I was situated, and hitting another contraction, they checked my baby's heartbeat. It was back to where it was supposed to be.

The strength I gained from that position was enough to be productive with my contractions and get him out. After only a few minutes of pushing, our long-awaited blessing was born—and in my arms. I laid there with him on my chest, just staring at this plump, newborn body covered in lanugo. I looked up at Bobby and saw him smiling back at me with tears welling in his eyes. I turned to see Linda wiping away tears, and I could hear the emotions in Tina's voice behind me. Our son didn't cry right away, and I was catching my breath from the intense labor. Tina reached across me to rub his back to coax my baby to take a breath . . . it worked. He let out a cry and my heart overflowed with joy as I felt the oxytocin high rush over me.

I began to laugh. He was here! Our much-anticipated child was finally here. He was more beautiful than anything we could have imagined. Our very own, full-term, newborn baby to hold and love. He had the biggest blue eyes and a lot of strawberry blonde hair that covered his body. He fit perfectly swaddled in the crook of my arm.

I got to watch Bobby hold his strong, whole, healthy, lively baby. I felt tears trickling down. It was the third time I had witnessed this picture of him with our child, but this time, instead of tears of sorrow, they were tears of great joy.

I was able to get our baby to nurse, and then I took an herbal bath with him so we were both clean and presentable.

Bobby called our families to share the good news that our baby was born and both he and I were healthy. Soon, the quaint birth center was overflowing with family and friends who had come to see our perfect baby boy. Everyone gathered as we prayed and anointed him with oil, celebrating our triumph and gift.

We left the birth center that night—finally as a family of three. We stayed at my parents' house one last night. While moving our belongings to the new place, we strategically kept anything we might need at my parents' place in case our son made his arrival before we could get situated in our new home.

The next day, my grandparents came to visit; they had been coming through the area from a vacation. This child being a boy was an amazing gift in and of itself. Not that girls aren't special, obviously, but there were no other boys in the family with the loss of my baby brother and Enoch. This little boy was just what my family needed.

After my grandparents left, Bobby gathered some family members and close friends to move our final things from my parents' house and then unpack our stuff. That evening, Bobby loaded our new baby and me in the truck and we made our way across town to our new home. We drove up to makeshift yard decorations and Bobby's family cheering for us in our front yard.

We were home. Our home. Not completely unpacked, but we were moved in as a family of three.

You may be wondering what we named this new baby boy. You may have guessed. Without further ado . . .

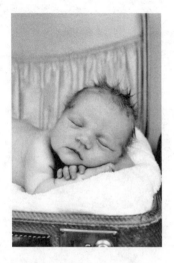

Bobby Lynn Pope IV

a.k.a. "Buddy"
Birthplace: Rockwall, Texas
Born: March 16, 2012, 7:54 p.m.
Weight: 8 pounds
Length: 21.5 inches

For God so loved the world that he gave his
one and only Son, that whoever believes in him
shall not perish but have eternal life.

—JOHN 3:16

Fourteen

I waited patiently for the Lord; he turned to me and heard
my cry.
He lifted me out of the slimy pit, out of the mud and mire;
he set my feet on a rock and gave me a firm place to stand.
He put a new song in my mouth, and a hymn of praise to
our God.
Many will see and fear and put their trust in the Lord
—Psalm 40:1-3

When I reflect back to my childhood and teenage years, never did I wonder what the journey to motherhood would look like. I only knew I wanted children. I never felt destined for the corporate world or chasing a career. My biggest dream in life was to marry my high school sweetheart and be a mother to our children.

It wasn't until Buddy was born that I fully grasped what I had been missing. What it was like to be fully responsible for a child and have him depend on me for his every need.

How sweet that early time was. I didn't mind—not one iota—the moonlight awakenings, or that he wanted to be in my arms a lot. I knew I might be spoiling him, but after everything I had been through, I didn't want to put him down.

While Bobby was away at work, Buddy and I spent countless hours nestled up on the couch streaming movies and TV shows. Often, I stayed up late sewing with Buddy by my side, then slept in until noon the following day. When Bobby came home, he'd join me in basking in the presence of this tiny being we had been blessed with. He was a gift, and we didn't want to miss any moments we didn't need to.

It was a dream come true, and to have that time together is something I completely cherished and hope to never forget. We were content.

After the first year of Buddy's life, we knew we wanted more kids. I had baby fever bad, and there was no denying it. I experienced how fleeting that baby stage of life was, and I didn't like it slipping through my fingers.

Bobby and I also revisited the idea of adoption, even strongly looking into adopting internationally from The Congo. We had started fundraising, but soon that dream was laid to rest as adoptions from The Congo were quickly declining—and I found myself pregnant again.

Bobby's brother Josh, and his fiancé Molly, were getting married soon, so we decided to keep this special secret between us and my midwife so they could have their moment to shine. Just after their wedding, Bobby had to turn around and leave for work, this time in Oklahoma. When he left, I started cramping and had some light bleeding. Tina had me come to the birth center to draw blood for testing my hormones. She recommended I start taking progesterone as a precaution.

The spotting lasted a few days and eventually turned into a miscarriage that sent me to the hospital.

Here's how that happened. It was naptime, so I laid down with Buddy when I felt something—and it was more than spotting—make me think I should go to the bathroom. In an instant, my light bleeding had turned into heavy bleeding. I was in denial. Bobby wasn't home, and we hadn't told our families yet. I was losing so much blood that I found it best to stand in the bathtub since I couldn't find a pad thick enough to hold it all. Realizing things were getting serious, I called Tina and asked her advice. She said, "If you are filling up a maxi-pad in less than an hour, then you are hemorrhaging and need to go to the hospital."

We ended the call, and I leaned against the wall of the tub with Buddy on the tile completely oblivious to what was going on. Things were too serious to drive myself. I was slowly becoming lightheaded. For a moment, I considered not telling anyone, but I knew that was an awful idea. I needed help, but I was also so embarrassed. I swallowed my pride and called my mom. To tell her in the same breath that I was pregnant again and miscarrying . . . well, this was a phone call I never thought I'd make. But I had no choice. I needed her help to get to the emergency room.

I then had to make the same call to my mother-in-law, to ask if she would come get Buddy. Without hesitation, both moms came right over. Michele, my mother-in-law, arrived first and worked on getting the spare car seat installed in her vehicle. I watched her from the front door as she tried to use the latches. They were buried deep in the seat and she could not find them. She asked a question about the car seat, and I was too weak to answer her. The sun was beating down; the Texas heat was nearly enough to knock me out. I recommended she take my car for her trip.

I saw my mom pull up behind her, grabbed my purse, and asked her to open the door as I made my way to her truck while guarding my eyes from the sun. The air conditioner was blasting, and I told Mom to take me to the nearest emergency room. I knew it was too serious to make the drive to Dallas by ourselves. With the cool air, I began to loosen up and not be so tense from the heat of the sun. I must have relaxed a little too much, because the next thing I knew, my mom was frantically shaking me with her right arm and screaming my name. The A/C was freezing cold, and though there was no music coming through the speakers, lyrics from a certain song by Emerson Drive—about how I should be sleeping, but instead I'm left "pacing and retracing"—were in my head. Why? I had no idea, but as I came to consciousness again I thought that's what was happening.

I had fainted in front of my mom while she was navigating her way through my neighborhood. I woke as she was nearing the farm-to-market road that would take us to the ER. My mom asked if I was OK and did her best to keep me talking. She then thought it best to call ahead to the ER and give them a heads-up on our arrival. About five minutes later, we pulled to the curb and my mom ran in to get someone. They came out with a wheelchair and rolled me straight through the lobby to an observation room.

They gathered the usual information, checked vitals, and asked me to pee in a cup. I was able to make my way to the bathroom. As I was sitting there, trying to will the liquid to leave my body, I felt myself fading away again. Thinking I should lay down, I pulled my pants up and started walking toward the bed. All of a sudden, I opened my eyes to my mom and several of the hospital staff asking me how my head felt . . . while I was lying in the doorway to the bathroom.

I had fainted again.

With the help of several people, I made it back to bed. They helped change me into a hospital gown and put a giant square pad underneath my bottom to soak up any more blood I was losing. Good thing, at this point, the bleeding had slowed.

Michele showed up once I was situated and sat next to my mother by the bed. She had dropped Buddy off at her house and put someone else in the family in charge of watching him so she could be with me. The three of us talked for a few minutes until a doctor came in to give me an update on the game plan. It was obvious I needed more attention than they could give, she said, so I would be transported via ambulance to Lake Point Medical Center in Rowlett. Once I was updated, the doctor felt I needed a "come to Jesus talk" about the type of medical care I should be seeking. In front of my mom and mother-in-law, she let me know that with my history of a stillborn, pre-term labor, anencephaly, and amniotic band syndrome, I was high risk and never should have used a midwife. She told me that if I had been her patient in the delivery of Buddy, she would have induced me early and not let me go past my due date.

I held my tongue, but I'll be honest, I was completely annoyed with her and the way she conducted herself. I'm sure after recognizing what was sent to her was from a midwife, she briefly scanned my documents, found the trigger words that stuck out to her, and had her mind made up—no ifs, ands, or buts. If only she had taken the time to actually study my history, she would have known that just because I preferred using a midwife didn't mean I was an idiot. My midwives and I were extremely thorough and did not handle my care lightly. Every decision I made regarding my care had a well-thought-out and researched reason behind it. If we saw fit to see a doctor, that is what I did. Not to mention that the giant piece of information she disregarded was that after my first two losses, I went on to have a fairly easy pregnancy, carrying past my due date—with no threats of pre-term labor—and saw a perinatologist regularly with sonograms and stress tests. Buddy had passed with flying colors every time, and I delivered with a midwife out of a hospital with no complications.

As I've said before, I know my decisions aren't popular. Starting about ten years ago, I didn't think this would be my preferred method of care either. As I've navigated through this journey, I've found that if I can use a midwife, I will. It's what I prefer. As you've seen through this book, midwives are simply different. Most midwives work their schedule in such a way that it allows them to build a relationship with their clients, one in which the mothers feel comfortable sharing their needs and concerns, knowing they will be heard. When I've needed a doctor, I've been fortunate enough to find docs who treated me with the same decency as my midwives. I have respected those doctors, made a point to stay in contact with them, and recommended them to others time and time again. They are some of the good ones.

Maybe the doctor in the ER that day actually cared, but the delivery of her message was not conveyed—nor received—in the way she no doubt wanted. I'm sure there are people who agree 100 percent with what she said to me, and I'm OK with that. There is some truth to what she said, but pregnancy cannot be put in a box, and it is not the same for every woman every time. Each and every pregnancy is different. I'm not saying disregard a woman's history; I'm saying take it into consideration and plan accordingly. Women are not cattle to be herded through a pregnancy without regard to the fact that they are all different. What matters to them should not be disregarded.

I failed miserably at the ol' "smile and nod" response to the doctor that day. I fumbled through it out of courtesy, but I'm sure she saw through my poker face. I knew it wouldn't have done any good to challenge her thinking. To her I was some ignorant girl who was too naive to know better . . . what did I have on her as a doctor? At least, that's what I felt coming from her, and besides, I didn't have the strength.

After the doctor left, I never saw her again. It wasn't long until the paramedics were there to transport me to a larger hospital. Two men about the same age as myself walked in my room with a stretcher. I was already bashful in their presence, but then the nurse told me they would be lifting me up off the bed onto the stretcher. If there was any ounce of color left in my complexion, it left.

I was mortified and, in front of everyone, yelled, "No! They are not picking me up!"

The nurse was taken back and asked, "Why?" Clearly, she was in work mode, and bodily fluids and bare private parts didn't bother her.

I realized I was just going to have to be frank. I reminded

her in front of everyone, "My backside is exposed, I'm bleed-ing everywhere, and they are men."

She assured me it would be OK. These men see stuff like this all the time and don't think anything about it, she said. I buried my ego and bowed my head so I wouldn't make eye contact with the men as they moved me.

I was stable and it was getting late, so I said goodbye to my mom and Michele. Bobby was on his way in from out of town and would meet me at the other hospital.

The men loaded me in the ambulance and we headed out. I felt it necessary to occupy my mind by aimlessly scrolling Facebook. It was working. I was in another world, looking at the highlight reels of other people's lives, and forgetting where I was at—in the middle of a miscarriage, and forced to surren-der my modesty.

Over the time of our ride, my concern about these men seeing me in a vulnerable state slipped away. They really didn't seem fazed by my appearance and just saw me as a regular person. When we arrived at the hospital, it was a lot easier letting them transfer me into another bed, even though I still didn't like it. We said our goodbyes, and they were on their way again.

The nurse came in, asked for all my information, drew blood for testing, hooked me up to fluids, and gave me a pill to help stop the bleeding. About an hour later, Bobby arrived. It was already late, so we had to wait till morning to be seen by a doctor.

It felt good to see Bobby again and was comforting to have him back at my side. It hadn't been officially confirmed, but we knew it: we were losing another baby. One who had already made a dent in our lives, including moving our thoughts toward beginning to see ourselves as a family of four.

Those plans had been violently derailed as we laid next to each other in the hospital bed that night. I replayed the day's events and how mortifying each step was . . . being home alone with Buddy while I bled out . . . calling our mothers to break the news . . . and passing out not once but twice in front of my mom.

There may have been symptoms of a miscarriage for a few days, but being as early as I was in my pregnancy, there wasn't anything that could be done to stop it. We were sad, but it was different this time. We didn't feel broken like we had before. We knew everything was going to be OK; we would make it through this just fine.

The next morning, we had a sonogram and met with the doctor. She confirmed I was losing a baby about seven weeks along, and she asked to check my cervix. She explained that usually when a woman hemorrhages from a miscarriage her cervix is not dilating enough to let the baby pass. The uterus just knows it needs to push a baby out and clamps or contracts down in order to do so. But when the cervix isn't dilating enough, the uterus is only able to push blood out, over and over. She let me know that just because this happened to me once, it didn't mean I would experience it again. This could happen to anyone, she said, and there was no way to prevent it.

The doctor informed me that if this was indeed the case, I would need a D&C—dilation and curettage—to remove everything inside my uterus.

Bobby left to grab something to eat while the doctor checked my cervix. She found the entire sack of my baby sitting at the entrance of my uterus. She pulled it out, fitting it in the palm of her hand. I raised up, in awe, and asked if I could see my baby. Appearing disturbed at my question, she looked up at me and said, "No, you don't want to see it." She handed my baby to the nurse and told her to take it to pathology for testing. I questioned why, but she insisted that I wouldn't want to because the baby had been lost so early.

If there was a pivotal moment of sadness, it was right then. I didn't think I would get to see my baby, and I was OK with that. It's the nature of an early miscarriage. But then I saw an opportunity directly in front of me. That was my baby—but I wasn't allowed to see it. Since the birth of Enoch, I've heard several women, usually significantly older than me, open up about their losses during pregnancy. They would deliver these babies, as I did with Enoch and Mary Alice, but the medical staff thought it best to not let the mothers see their child. I would think how awfully sad that must have been for them. Now, obviously, times have changed and you can usually see your baby. I had just witnessed a glimpse of what it was like for these other mothers. Just like that, on the decision of another, I wasn't granted the chance to see my baby.

I backed down and let it be.

The good news was, I didn't need a D&C after all. Another sonogram confirmed that the doctor got everything left in my uterus. She ordered two blood transfusions for me and said I would need to stay another night.

The transfusions made a difference and I checked out the next day. Bobby took me home. When we arrived, I showed him the bathtub with the dried blood lining the tub. It was a hard to sight to see. He turned the water on, grabbed a rag, and cleaned it up. My eyes watered watching him clean up after me, and I told him I was sorry for leaving such a mess.

In a low, soft voice, he said, "Don't worry about it. I've got it. It's OK."

This was the one of the only times I remember crying over our miscarriage. It wasn't so much about the miscarriage as it was about Bobby's love for me. In sickness and in health.

We decided to go ahead and name our child even though we didn't get the chance to meet him or her. Since we had lost two babies before, it was important to me that if I ever had a miscarriage I wanted my baby to still have a name. A few years before, I came up with the name Jordan, after the Jordan River. A name that fit well for a boy or girl.

I had the blood transfusions, but I still felt very weak. Upon leaving the hospital, the doctor who oversaw me said to call her office if we had any questions or concerns. We found ourselves concerned with my lack of strength, and I wanted to be seen by her again. We called her office and explained, but they couldn't get me in right away. It was going to be a couple of days. So I took to the Internet to find ways to get my blood count up. Bobby drove me to the natural food store so I could stock up on supplements to help increase my blood count.

I also found myself calling my first midwife, Kelly. I remembered her telling me about a time she hemorrhaged, so I wanted to inquire about her recovery. She told me it was normal to still feel weak and that it would actually take several weeks for my blood count to get back up and about three months for my body to be normal again. Kelly said I needed to be careful going out in public because I was more susceptible to illness with my immune system down. She recommended I eat lots of green vegetables and rest.

It felt good catching up with her. It had been a while. Her soft, motherly voice put me at ease as she related with this season of my life.

Before long I was feeling like myself again. A little at a time, my strength returned. We made our way through Thanksgiving, and Christmas was approaching. And those familiar sensations of pregnancy crept back in. Since my body was still recovering, we weren't trying to get pregnant. Our plan was to wait one more cycle. By now, I knew what pregnancy felt like, though, so I decided to take a test to confirm. To no surprise, it showed positive. We were expecting again. I was very early, almost five weeks.

We told our parents and siblings as soon as we found out. After last time, we did not want to wait longer than necessary. I got in touch with Tina right away. To be safe, she recommended I start the progesterone immediately.

Christmas Eve was traditionally spent with the Pope side of the family at Bobby's parents' house. Just about everyone from Bobby's dad's side of the family gathers and we celebrate the birth of Jesus. We have a huge dinner, play dominos, conduct a white elephant-style gift opening, sing Christmas carols, and listen as someone reads a passage of Jesus' birth from the Bible.

This year was no different. We all came together, enjoyed catching up with one another, and spread the good news of us expecting another baby. Toward the end of the night, I felt some light menstrual-like cramps. I whispered to Bobby what I was feeling, and we silently prayed. I decided to take it easy on the couch, snuggling up next to Bobby as we watched our son play with his cousins on the floor. I was able to compartmentalize the fear of another miscarriage and put it away. I knew there was nothing that could be done if I was miscarrying, and I didn't want to lose this joyous moment of watching our precious toddler giggle and play with others his age. It was one of those moments we looked forward to for so long. There was no way I was going to let Satan steal it in the form of fear.

At the end of the night, we went home and nestled in bed to rest up for Christmas Day.

Christmas arrived and we woke up extra early to be with my family to eat breakfast and open each other's gifts. Buddy woke with a slight fever, but we still decided to spend the morning at my parents' house. He cuddled with Bobby and me, sleeping off and on. I still had a lingering, dull ache in my lower abdomen, but again, there was nothing I could do about it except take it as easy as possible.

After we left my parents' house, we headed back to Bobby's parents to open presents with his immediate side of the family. It wasn't five minutes after arriving there that that dreadful, familiar feeling come over me and made me want to go to the bathroom and check to make sure everything was OK. I quietly slipped away to the nearest restroom. I held my breath as I looked down to see spotting. A pit in my stomach appeared and I felt my face get flush. I knew what was happening, and it frustrated me. I pulled Bobby away from his brothers and took him into the laundry room. I told him it was happening again; I was having a miscarriage. Tears pooled in my eyes and I silently yelled, "*Why?!* Why do I keep having to go through this?! Why is this happening to me?! I'm so tired of it!" He pulled me close and I let the tears fall. "I don't know," Bobby said. "I'm sorry. I hate this too."

His reaction was enough to help me pull myself back together so I wouldn't ruin everyone's day. We left the laundry room and did our best to remain calm and collected. It wasn't working, though. Everyone felt the tension in the room as we began to open presents. It was my turn to open a gift. Michele held our sleeping Buddy in her arms. I opened a small present that she had picked out from James Avery, a charm. It was so thoughtful and fit perfectly with my collection. But I couldn't play cool anymore. I started crying. Bobby decided it was needed, it was time, to break the ice. He told them what I was dealing with. In that moment the burden left me as I didn't have to deal with it alone anymore. I explained a little more and assured everyone it was nothing like last time, but that I was pretty certain I was losing another baby.

As relieving as it was to get that off our chests, there was one more thing I needed to do. I wanted to tell my parents. It was so awful how the news was broken for them the last time I miscarried, and I didn't want it to happen that way again. I grabbed my phone and snuck off to the laundry room to let them know. I was able to tell them both and gave my assurance I would keep them updated on any changes.

When I returned to the living room with everyone else, Michele informed us how hot Buddy felt. He was becoming lethargic. We checked his temperature. The thermometer read 104. We gathered the children's fever reducer medicine, a wet rag, and got him a bottle of water with vitamin C.

Michele offered to continue holding him. I didn't mind. I

knew when her boys were sick, she didn't care about anything but catering to their every need—whether it be pressing a wet cloth to their head or rocking them as they slept. She was a child who fell ill a lot, and though she was one of nine kids, her mother took the time to meet her needs as well. Usually, I would have held Buddy, but knowing I was miscarrying, it was nice to have the extra support.

Slowly, Buddy came back around as his fever faded and he no longer needed medicine. We finished opening gifts, relaxed the rest of the day, and kept in touch with my parents. It was not the way we anticipated Christmas Day going, but I still remember the joy I felt that evening. I remember voicing what I was feeling in my heart . . . that despite what was going on, it was still a good Christmas because I got to spend the entire day with the people I loved most.

First thing the next morning, I called Tina to let her know I believed I was losing another baby. She recommended I get an appointment with Dr. Payne from Baylor to confirm. After ending our call, I reached Payne's office and they were able to get me in the next day.

On the 27th, I loaded up Buddy and made the drive into Dallas. I walked into a waiting room full of women with nice round bellies. It pained me to see them, but I swallowed the hurt and focused on how adorable Buddy was.

Soon, I was called back. The nurse checked my vitals and then directed me into the sonogram room, handing me a paper blanket to wrap around my waist.

Dr. Payne came in and I briefly caught him up on what I had been dealing with. He turned on the machine and checked for a baby. There was none. He pointed out where there had been a baby and explained that my body had already passed it. He apologized, recommended I wait a cycle before trying again, and then left.

The nurse in the room with us told me she was sorry for my loss and seemed sincerely bothered at having to witness this. I assured her that it really was OK. I had learned to not spill my guts about my past, so I kept it short and sweet. "Thank you," I said. "It really is OK. I'll be all right."

I appreciated her heart, and as I've found out through the years, Dr. Payne brings out the best in his nurses. He sees people as actual souls, recognizing that each person is made in the image of God and deserves to be treated as such. His kind demeanor flows over to his nurses and then to his patients, and this makes for a peaceful experience regardless of the circumstances.

I called Bobby as I left the doctor's office. He was back at work. I filled him in with confirmation of what we already knew. We had lost a fourth baby.

It seemed awful, but the only time I was heavily burdened by the weight of another loss was those few minutes between when I saw the spotting and when we opened up to family about it. I knew this baby was a gift; it was a surprise we weren't expecting. We knew my body was still recovering, so this pregnancy ending in a miscarriage did not come as a total shock. We had just found out we were expecting at barely five weeks gestation. If I hadn't taken a test so soon, we probably wouldn't have known I was pregnant again.

But I did, and with the knowledge of another child, we decided it deserved a name as well. In honor of losing our tiny baby on Christmas Day, we gave the name Noel.

As the new year began, I had a feeling it was going to be a good one. Another cycle came and went and it was now the middle of February. And then, as expected, those old familiar signs crept back in signaling it was time for a test. Bobby and Buddy were in the kitchen cooking dinner when I snuck off to our bathroom. I grabbed an extra test I had from under the sink and took it. Within minutes it came back positive. I smiled and knew this time would be different. I reached under the sink again for the bottle of progesterone and applied it where it was recommended. I walked out, set that bottle on the kitchen counter, and said, "Looks like I'm going to be using this again."

Now . . . my smooth hint wasn't received the way I planned in my head. Bobby did not remember what the bottle was for. I explained: "I just took a test. I'm pregnant again."

With a grin, he replied, "All right. Cool!"

Fifteen

A month later, in March of 2014, we sold our house. During the process of selling, Bobby lost his job. He accepted another job, but because of the employment change we were not able to get a loan for another house. When we closed, the housing market was on its way up. We gained a considerable amount of money and decided to invest it in some land out east. Bobby, Buddy, and I moved into a two-bedroom, one-bath home. We downsized our living space tremendously, moving into a rental home owned by my in-laws.

Through our losses, Bobby and I learned to make the most of what we had. We didn't know how long we would live in that house, but we knew we would be bringing another child home to this new place. While Bobby was at work, I unpacked our belongings and figured out what items we really needed and put the rest in storage. I created a space that worked for us and found beauty in the simplicity and character of the home.

There wasn't enough room for a nursery, so I found space

in a corner of our room for a Pack 'n Play and created space in Buddy's closet for the new baby's clothes.

I had been in touch with Tina about this pregnancy. She expressed that she thought it best to see Dr. Payne through about the first fourteen weeks just to make sure everything was healthy and viable. I began seeing Dr. Payne right away. Every appointment went smoothly, and I even got to peek at our baby on his sonogram machine a couple of times.

Dr. Payne did make note that I had placenta previa, a condition in which the placenta covers the cervix, but at fourteen weeks he gave me the OK to continue care with Tina.

I reminded him of the previa, thinking he had forgotten.

Smiling, he nodded. "Yes, I know," he said. "I'm not concerned with it. If it doesn't move off your cervix, I know you'll be back. I'm confident it will move, though."

Though I was pleased with my experience with Dr. Payne, I was happy to be back in my comfort zone of a birth center setting.

Because of the placenta previa, I saw a perinatologist for my twenty-week ultrasound at Baylor Hospital's Fetal Care Center. At this appointment, they looked closely at our baby from head to toe, checking all the details, including the placement of the placenta. This was also the appointment in which we would find out our baby's gender.

Through this entire pregnancy, Bobby did not want to

talk about names for our child. He was set on having another boy; he didn't want to fathom raising a girl. I knew him well enough to just let him be; his mind was made up (for now). Deep down, I knew I was having a girl. I had this instinctual notion, even before we conceived this child, that she would be a girl. Long before I became pregnant with this baby, I knew I wanted Joy to be part of her name. After I became pregnant with her, I heard the name Lucy and instantly knew that was the one. She would bring so much light and joy to our family.

The name was an instant favorite to anyone I shared it with, but I didn't share this name (that I felt God had laid on my heart) with Bobby until the day of our sonogram appointment. He was in town, so he was able to join me at the visit. On our way to Dallas, I brought up the name discussion. Maybe it wasn't the best time for this, but I didn't care. I was excited either way, and yet I was still confident this appointment would confirm what I already knew.

"I know we haven't discussed this," I said, "but I feel it is necessary since we are about to find out if I'm carrying a boy or a girl. What names do you have in mind?"

"Stoney for a boy," Bobby shared, "because I think it's a cool name. I don't have a girl name picked out because I know it's a boy."

He was curious what I had come up with, so I shared. "Lucy Joy for a girl," I said. "I haven't decided on a boy name because I'm pretty positive it's a girl."

For a moment, we laughed at each other's stubbornness. But then I said I wanted his honest opinion.

"What do you think about the girl name I told you?" I asked.

"I think it's nice. I like it," was all Bobby said.

His reaction to the name Lucy Joy was like a confirmation,

even before the sonogram, that the child I was carrying was indeed a girl. There had been a few small hints or signs I felt were from God along the way showing me who this little being was. And I didn't pick the name out; He did. For my husband to agree to this name so easily, without hesitation, on our way to the gender-reveal sonogram was like icing on a very pink cake. Now all I needed was for the doctor to cut a slice of that cake and show us the color.

When we entered the exam room, the doctor asked if we wanted to find out the gender. As quickly as the doctor asked, Bobby responded. "Yes, we do. We ain't doing no gender-reveal party or waiting to find out when the baby is born. To be honest, if we waited to find out when the baby gets here, it would take me a while before I was happy if the baby turned out to be a girl. Better find out now so I can get used to the idea."

You should have seen the look on the doctor's face. Her jaw dropped and her eyes widened. She could not believe the obstinacy Bobby had just expressed. He had been in the oil field industry a few years now. These people aren't called roughnecks for no reason. That roughness had rubbed off on him, and at times he had no problem sharing how he really felt.

I wasn't bothered one bit by his answer. I got a good kick out of it and began to laugh. I could tell the doctor wasn't too sure about him, so I tried to put her at ease. "Don't mind him. He is serious, but he'll be fine. To answer your question, yes. We would like to know the gender."

She breathed a sigh of relief and we went on with our appointment.

I mentioned our concern with the placenta previa, so she checked that first. I also requested she tell us everything she was looking at and if things weren't appearing as they should. We were thrilled to receive the good news that the placenta had moved up the wall of my uterus and was no longer a threat to the pregnancy. She worked her way around our baby's body, studying every detail. She made her way to our child's private part and officially confirmed it: we were expecting a girl.

I was on cloud nine at the news. The appointment couldn't have gone better. The doctor left the room and we gathered our things. Our daughter's profile was left up on the big monitor. I was giddy with excitement and made Bobby and Buddy, who was along with us, huddle in front of the screen for a selfie. "Our first picture as a family of four!" I exclaimed.

"You're so cheesy," Bobby moped.

"Ha ha. I know no one likes an 'I told you so,' but I told you so," I said, pointing at him in the most childish manner. "Never contradict a mother's instinct of her baby's gender."

Bobby was genuinely crushed at the news, but I didn't care. I knew that once our girl was born, he would fall head over boots in love with her.

You'd think after everything we'd been through, it wouldn't matter one way or the other as long as the baby was healthy—but it did. The thought of raising a girl scared Bobby. It still does today. Just this last week, in writing this book, after he walked out from tucking our daughter into bed, he said, "Man, I have no clue if I'm doing anything right with her." I agreed that it is hard. "Yeah, she's totally different than Buddy," I said. Something tells me he's doing all right, though. Last night he went back into her room after hearing her crying from bed and helped her put a diaper on her baby doll because she didn't want it to sleep naked. It is pure sweetness to see the two of them interact. She has the ability to soften him in a way only a daughter can.

As we neared the thirty-week mark, we decided to have another peek at our baby. Tina's sono tech was coming to her birth center for a day of appointments, so we saw this as another opportunity to look at our girl.

It had been four years since I had a sonogram at Tina's birth center. I wondered if she still used the same sonographer. I showed up for my appointment and, even though times had changed and things were different this time, anxiety set in when I saw the same tech I had seen with Mary Alice's pregnancy. My heart raced and I was jittery, but I reminded myself that it wasn't 2010 anymore. Things would be OK.

Tina reintroduced us; the technician remembered me. I'm sure even from her point of view that moment in time is one that has remained with her. To put us all at ease, I was able to show her how life had turned around for us and I introduced her to Buddy. Getting to show him off put me at ease more than anything, and now I was ready to see my little girl.

As had become my practice, I requested the technician share with me what she was looking at when she saw it, and to let me know if something was normal or not. She shook her head in understanding and we started the scan.

Everything was checking out just as it should, but then my heart started pounding and my throat tightened when I noticed her lingering the wand over my daughter's face.

In a panic, I asked, "What are you looking at?"

She quickly reassured me. "Everything really is OK," she

said, "but I see something next to her eye. I'll be right back. I'm going to get Tina."

She left and I felt fear try to make its way back in. I prayed, "Lord, please wash your peace over me. Please let everything be OK."

Soon enough, Tina and the sonographer reentered. Tina made sure to be upbeat and positive to keep me calm.

The sonographer grabbed the wand and slid it over my stomach once more.

"See, right there," she said to Tina. "I thought it might be a fluke, but it's not going away."

Tina nodded in understanding, then turned to explain. "Lucy has a cyst between her eye and nose. It's a small, fluid-filled pocket that will probably go away on its own."

"Will I be able to deliver her here?" I asked.

"Yes," Tina said.

"It won't hinder her breathing?" I had to question a little further.

"No, it shouldn't," Tina answered. "But just to be safe, I'd like to have another sonogram with the perinatologist."

As we wrapped up the appointment, Tina made sure I knew how confident she was that Lucy would be fine. She reminded me that this was a different baby and a completely different scenario.

After I left the birth center, I made another appointment at the Fetal Care Center at Baylor. The earliest they could get me in was three weeks. I called Bobby to let him know all about this appointment. He didn't seem phased at the news; in fact, he seemed so preoccupied by work that it kept him from jumping headfirst into any emotions. I recognized this and felt it best not to try and force anything out of him. I asked him to pray that our baby would be completely healed and that my nerves would stay calm. He quickly agreed and began our talk with God.

Once he concluded the prayer, Bobby said, "Hey, don't worry about it. Everything will be just fine. Try not to think about it too much."

We decided to keep this concern to ourselves until we had more answers. We felt strong enough to carry this knowledge ourselves and did not want to burden our families again.

I knew Bobby was right. I would tell myself not to think about it, but living in a world such as we do, where we have answers at our fingertips, I couldn't let myself settle without knowing more. I took to the Internet, skimming one site after another for anything, but couldn't find any matches. I didn't like not knowing more about this cyst on my daughter's face.

I had to reach out to my first midwife, Kelly. Fully aware that she had been in the midwifery field for a while now, I wondered if she had come across something like this before. She had not, but she requested I send her a picture of my daughter's face. As it turns out, her son-in-law was in school studying to become a sono tech. She thought he or his professor might know. It would be a few days before I received an answer.

In the meantime, it didn't take long till I felt the same lie of fear sneak back into my mind that I had faced with Mary Alice . . . *What would she look like? Would she be beautiful?* It was so familiar—almost a comfortable feeling, being back in this space—but I fought it, knowing it wasn't good for me.

My father-in-law gave me his audio copy of Jase and Missy Robertson's book, *Happy, Happy, Happy*. The Robertson family has always intrigued me, so I was thrilled to get my hands on this book. I'd listen to it as I went to and from church, visiting family, or shopping. We lived about thirty minutes away from everything, so I had plenty of chance to listen.

One day I was headed out to run errands, so I turned the CD on to listen to the book. I thoroughly enjoyed Jase and Missy's story because I felt Bobby and I related to them so well. Jase is a bearded copy of my husband, with the same sense of logic and humor—they even hunt the same way. Jase is adamant that one must commit his whole body to lunge or dive toward a frog before it leaps away. My husband is the only other person I've known who is willing to give it his all like that.

As the book goes on, Jase speaks not only of the fun, light-hearted times in their lives, but also turns serious and shares about the hard stuff too. If you didn't know, Jase and Missy's daughter, Mia, was born with a cleft lip and palate. They were given the news of Mia's condition while Missy was pregnant, and to hear this rugged man share of their struggles hit home with me. At one point, listening, I lost it and was in full-blown, wailing tears as I drove down the interstate.

I was scared.

I wanted my daughter to be perfect.

I wanted to know she would be OK and able to breathe on her own.

I pulled over in the parking lot of an outlet mall and called Tina. I shared with her just how scared I was. She listened and then spoke words of encouragement over me. She expressed that she had no doubt that Lucy would be just fine, and she reminded me that if she wasn't so sure, she would let me know. We talked for about forty-five minutes while she consoled me and concluded in prayer.

I was much better after our conversation. She heard me and was there for me. She didn't mind taking time out of her busy day to listen, and it meant so much to me.

Though I was more levelheaded about Lucy's cyst, I still wanted to know more. I was tired of waiting. I took to the Internet again. This time, I found something I knew had to be her condition: a lacrimal duct cyst. It wasn't as serious as it appeared in her picture, and I was able to learn everything I wanted to know about it: that it would probably go away on its own, and, if not, it wouldn't be life-threatening, and surgery could fix it. I found pictures of babies born with this condition and prepared myself in case she was born with the cyst still in place. It didn't look horrible, maybe a little uncomfortable to the baby, and nothing that couldn't heal.

Soon after, I received a returned call from Kelly with an answer from her son. I told her what I had found and she laughed. "You won't believe this," she said. "His teacher showed it to the entire class and asked them to assess it. They unanimously, unofficially diagnosed it as a lacrimal duct cyst."

I thanked her for looking into it and shared that I was at peace about it. I was happy to hear that I was probably correct in my findings. I was finally confident everything would be OK.

My next appointment came and, when I entered the exam room, the doctor asked me why I was there. I explained the cyst that was found on my last sonogram and that we wanted to get a second opinion. I shared how I thought it may be a lacrimal duct cyst. I had forgotten my hard copy of the picture, but I had it on my phone. I shared it with him.

He zoomed in to study it for a moment, then said, "It may be nothing. Let's take a look."

He studied both eyes and found nothing. He zoomed in

and showed me there was no trace of a cyst on either eye. He chalked it up to a reflection the sonographer must have seen, and I sensed he felt we didn't know what we were talking about. I didn't care, and I knew it wasn't necessary to tell him about all the eyes that had seen the cyst. I was a happy girl! Our prayers had been answered. My daughter's lacrimal duct cyst was gone! Praise the Lord!

It was Sunday, November 9, 2014, and I was eight days past my due date. I was ready to hold my baby girl. Bobby had recently switched oil companies and was scheduled to leave that coming Tuesday to work offshore. We hoped Lucy would arrive before he left because there was no quick turnaround to return to shore once he was on the ship.

We woke up that morning with the intention of going to church, but while showering I mentioned I didn't want to see anyone. I was tired and didn't want to explain to people that I was indeed still pregnant. We decided to stay home, take the morning slow, and eat breakfast as a family.

That evening we drove to Grandma Zmolik's house so Bobby could visit with his uncles and watch the Cowboys game. I pretty much stayed put on the couch. I was feeling pretty worn and didn't want to move much.

After the game, Bobby and his brothers wanted to practice bow shooting, so we went to his parents' house. I stayed inside and visited with his mom. We didn't stay long.

As we were leaving, Michele looked at me and said, "I think you are going to have this baby tonight."

"Maybe," I replied.

While Bobby was loading up the car with our things, I

started to buckle Buddy in his car seat. An intense contraction hit me that took my breath away. I leaned against the car to endure the wave and catch my breath. When I finished, I told Bobby to finish buckling Buddy in.

On our way home I started timing the contractions. They came about every ten to fifteen minutes and were powerful.

In truth, I may have been in labor for several hours before that time but hadn't known it. I felt contractions, but chalked them up to Braxton Hicks since I had those all the time anyway. Once these contractions hit, I knew it was go-time.

At home I bounced on an exercise ball for a while. I decided to lie down and get some rest since it looked like it was going to be a long night. I called Tina while I laid there, informing her I was in labor and contractions were coming every five minutes. She told me to call when we were headed to the birth center.

About fifteen minutes later, Bobby walked past me to head to another part of the house when another contraction hit, one that magnified the pain even more than the others. This alarmed me, and I knew we had better get going. Bobby told me to get in the car and he would grab the bags and load up Buddy.

I made my way down the front steps, across the lawn, and opened the passenger door. A gust of blistering wind rushed by, carrying a huge chill with it, and another contraction hit. I stood there through it, focused on my breathing, and then got situated in the front seat.

As quick as possible, we were off. We lived in a very small town where the main streets are made of brick and the railroad rolls right through the middle. There was no going around those bumpy roads. I held on tight as Bobby carefully drove. I felt every single bump in that road as I endured another contraction.

Bobby called Tina and let her know we were on our way.

We made it through the stoplights of the next town, and then headed north to the birth center.

When we got there, I got out of the car and went straight inside to find Tina drawing the water in the copper tub of her "Yellow Rose" Room.

Since delivering Buddy, Tina had moved her birth center across the street into an old two-story house, renovating it to serve the needs of expecting and new mothers. The place is absolutely stunning, and its history is ironic. After it was a home, it was turned into a commercial property and served as a funeral home. Now, it was given another chance and had become a place of welcoming rather than goodbyes.

The new center housed three birthing suites: the Lone Star, the Bluebonnet, and the Yellow Rose rooms. Though it was the smallest, I chose the Yellow Rose Room because Tina designed it in honor of my first daughter, Mary Alice. She got the idea from the yellow rose on the door of my hospital room when I delivered her. A picture of Tina kissing Mary Alice, along with a one-dollar coin taped to the frame that I gave as payment for Buddy's pregnancy, resides above the newborn observing station in that room.

Tina asked how I was doing and I told her I just wanted to get in the tub. She reminded me that she would have to check my cervix first. I found myself grabbing the doorframe for support as I breathed through another contraction. When she checked me, much to the surprise of both of us, I was completely dilated, to a 10, and was 100 percent effaced. It was go-time—which meant I was allowed in the tub.

Bobby laid a sleeping Buddy down in another room and then sat next to my tub. He called our parents to inform them it was time. I worked through the contractions for a few more minutes. They were one on top of the other now, and I was miserable. In desperation, I said, "I need some help. I'm so tired."

Tina knew I was in transition and also noticed I was crowning. She turned to Bobby and said, "Hey, Daddy. You want to deliver?"

Birth did not scare Bobby anymore. He jumped up and said, "Uh, absolutely!"

She had him come to the other end of the tub, explained where to place his hands, and coached him through it. I knew how powerful my body was, so as I made those last few pushes I gave it everything I had. At one point, Tina even told me to slow down.

With each push, Bobby was able to tell me another feature of our little girl's face. This gave me the strength to keep going. Her head came, and then the shoulders. He lifted her out of the water and laid her on my chest. The Oxytocin kicked in the moment I laid eyes on her. "Oh my goodness! Oh my goodness!' I exclaimed. She was bigger than Buddy and had rolls around her thighs. She was definitely a girl!

She let out a gurgling cry. Tina opened a package that had a small tool for her to suck the fluid out of her lungs. It worked perfectly, and immediately Lucy Joy breathed on her own.

Once the cord stopped pulsing the rest of the blood into her body, Bobby had the honor of cutting it. Tina picked Lucy up with a towel and placed her in Bobby's arms. He was all giggles and thought she was just as precious as could be.

After I was situated in bed, Lucy was laid in my arms for us to try nursing. All she wanted to do was sleep, though. Bobby woke up Buddy to let him know his baby sister was here. He was scared of her at first, and it took him a few minutes to fully wake up. Once he realized I was holding a real, live baby, he became curious. He wanted to help me in any way possible. It warmed my heart to see the interaction between them. There was a newfound love for him as a big brother. One I didn't expect.

After midnight, family members strolled in to catch a glimpse of the newest member.

The dynamics of our family had changed. A girl had been added, and it was pure bliss.

Lucy Joy Pope
Born: November 9, 2014, 11:55 p.m.
Birthplace: Rockwall, Texas
Weight: 9 pounds, 2 ounces
Length: 19.5 inches

"For I know the plans I have for you," declares the Lord,
"plans to prosper you and not to harm you, plans
to give you a hope and a future."
—JEREMIAH 29:11

Lucy was such a easy baby. Bobby left for work just two days after she was born. That first night without him, I stayed up so late because I didn't know how to get two kids to bed. Eventually, we all tired out, and I quickly got the hang of our new life together.

After the first week or two, Lucy slept through the night; she was an excellent sleeper. She hardly cried, unless she was hungry. She was content with observing the world around her and rarely smiled. I knew the day would come when her shell would crack open and we'd get to see her sparkle shine.

It did. At about eleven months, she started walking. About a day or two after her first steps, Buddy was playing with toys on our coffee table. She grabbed one of them, and it sent him to react with a fit. Her eyes lit up and a smile appeared across her face. She took two steps to dart away with it, but fell and lost grip of the toy. Buddy picked it up and quickly made his way back to his perfectly lined toys.

Eleven-month-old Lucy just giggled. I smiled and thought to myself: *And there it is. She is her daddy's daughter.*

sixteen

We were so blessed to have the opportunity to raise these precious children. When Bobby was home, he did his best to make every moment count. We spent his off time as a family unit making memories together. I hated to have him away so much, but I recognized the sacrifice he was making in order to provide the best for our family. We knew the oil field wasn't the end goal, but it provided such an incredible opportunity to give us a leg up financially. Through his time in the field, he developed strong and productive work habits. This is something I am forever grateful for.

After Lucy's first year of life, Bobby walked away from the oil field and began working for his parents again. This allowed him to be home every night, and we gained a great deal of stability and consistency as a family. It was another answer to prayer.

As things drew closer to Lucy's second birthday, Bobby and I both caught baby fever again. Around Thanksgiving we were pleased to learn we were expecting. This news quickly became a joke between us as we knew exactly when this child was conceived. Happy Birthday, Bobby! He turned 30 on November 4.

Even before we conceived, we both strongly felt we were going to have a boy. Bobby had a dream about him, and his name was Casey. It's not a name either of us would have picked, but when he told me about it, the name just seemed to fit. I added the middle name James in honor of my brother, who passed away as a baby.

Linda, Tina's former apprentice, opened a birth center near the property we had bought and held onto for the past few years. We were in the beginning stages of building a home on this land when we found out we were going to have another baby. We decided to hire Linda for our care. We always enjoyed her company and knew she would be a good fit for where we were in life.

During this pregnancy, Bobby found an appreciation for this period of expectancy and everything that surrounded it. Not that he was exactly absent before, but now that he was home every night, his mind was consumed by our coming child more than the previous ones. He often commented on each milestone and would take a moment to acknowledge the small differences in life that came with each pregnancy.

We had routine sonograms as we did in the past. We discovered early on that I had placenta previa again. This time was more serious than with Lucy, and I was monitored well into the third trimester. It eventually moved off my cervix. This was a huge relief for everyone.

Another concern was that this little boy moved a lot. Not like a kick here, a jab there, but something like full body twists and turns. This was cute at first, but he continued to do so as my due date neared. He eventually settled in place, and I went on to have my quickest labor yet with him.

Sunday, July 23, 2017, the day before he was due, was spent like any other Sunday. We attended church, and that afternoon we planned on attending my cousin's son's birthday party. I joked with her earlier that weekend, saying, "we'll be there unless it's baby time."

After church Bobby, the kids, and I went to his parents' house for lunch and to wait until it was time for the party. After we ate, Buddy and I were in the bathroom so I could fix his hair when . . . the thought struck me that I might be in labor.

I called Linda to let her know. She wasn't certain that I was in labor, but recommended I come to the birth center.

As nonchalantly as possible, I told Bobby it was time for baby. We didn't tell anyone, and they assumed we were leaving for the party.

We left without any of our bags and went straight to the center. As we started down the road, it became apparent I was in labor. I experienced intense contractions every few minutes. We arrived at the birth center before Linda, but she had given us the code so we could head in and begin to settle. Linda and one of her apprentices arrived shortly after; eventually, another apprentice came as well. Once she arrived, Bobby left with the kids to grab our bags from the house. When he left, he called our parents and let them know where we were.

Linda got the water ready and let me slip in to relax. The contractions escalated, quickly, and I began to wonder if Bobby was going to make it back in time.

He and the kids arrived soon enough. Buddy came rushing in the room to see me, but I was not quite the same person he remembered—transition was upon me. Buddy was nervous and wanted to keep his distance while Lucy became little mama and wanted to make sure I was OK. I'll never forget the feeling of immense pain and then having a tiny, soft hand press gently against my arm to comfort me.

Buddy and Lucy were sent to the other room, which I was so thankful for. I became tired and asked for help. It meant one thing: transition. It was so exhausting, and just about the time I felt I couldn't handle any more of it, my body started pushing on its own. No lie. I had heard about women's bodies instinctively knowing how to do this, but I had never experienced it. Sounds crazy, I know. It excited me, because I knew the end was near. Just like with Lucy, Bobby leaned over the tub and caught our baby. The placenta quickly followed and, much to our surprise—or not—a true knot appeared in the cord.

Looking back through pictures you can see the Oxytocin bug hit Bobby instantly while I laid back to catch my breath. Casey was the easiest med-free birth I've experienced, but he was also the fastest, and this left me breathless.

My recovery after the delivery was a little slow. We stayed for a while so Linda and the other midwives could monitor my vitals and administer fluids. I was so thankful for their close care as they watched over me. Once again, I was amazed at these women. They worked together seamlessly as if they had been doing this their entire lives. I felt like a queen with everyone selflessly waiting on me hand and foot. Their acts of service that night are gifts I will always cherish.

Casey James Pope

Born: July 23, 2017, 5:58 p.m.
Birthplace: Kaufman, Texas
Weight: 7 pounds, 4 ounces
Length: 20.5 inches

Every good and perfect gift is from above, coming down from the Father of the heavenly lights, who does not change like shifting shadows. He chose to give us birth through the word of truth, that we might be a kind of firstfruits of all he created.

—JAMES 1:17, 18

We learned early on that life isn't always easy. It isn't always going to transpire as we hope. But childlike faith was instilled in Bobby and me when we were in our youth. Once our faith was rocked, we questioned, but to believe God had something remarkable for us, we had to put action to our belief, even when it hurt. We learned how precious life was, including our own, and have not wanted our moments to pass us by . . . even when life seemed grim.

We are never promised tomorrow, so we've found ourselves wanting to make each day count. It isn't easy, and we still struggle, but we have found that the joy of the Lord is our strength. We have learned that no matter the circumstances, we can always hold to His promises . . . and choose joy.

Abiding in Joy

There is a profound difference between happiness and joy.

Our Founding Fathers stated that the pursuit of happiness was endowed to us by our Creator—notice that they did not say that happiness was endowed by our Creator. They understood that happiness cannot be captured and held. It is fleeting and completely dependent on the circumstances surrounding the emotion.

If all is going well, you are happy. If you are pleasantly surprised, you are happy. All it takes is a discouraging word, a sad memory, a traumatic event—and happiness flees. In a matter of minutes (or even seconds) euphoric happiness can reach the depths of despair.

Joy, on the other hand, is deep and abiding. It is the unyielding belief that, no matter the circumstances, God is all powerful, and well able to bring you through those difficult times as certainly as dawn will follow darkness. It is surrendering your will to the will of the only One who is able to carry you when your legs fall out from under you.

Joy is peace in your soul when your heart is breaking; a gentle smile forming on your lips as tears are rolling down your cheeks; the sweet victory of passing a wrenching test and realizing it has become a testimony.

The joy of the Lord is our strength and passes all human understanding.

Aunt Darla

From Bobby

The loss of our children was and is the hardest thing I've gone through. The pain of our losses was so deep it physically hurt to cry. I knew there had to be an end at some point, so I would tell myself to hold on until I got to the other side of the trial. The only way I knew to hang in there was to do what I had been taught: to keep my feet firmly planted in my belief in Jesus.

I didn't understand why our babies weren't surviving, and I didn't like it. I kept thinking: *How does this make sense with what I believe?* Yet I knew there was an explanation. Even though I didn't understand, I refused to deny my Lord.

I don't believe God was holding us or shielding us through our experiences. He allowed us to go through these trials on our own two feet, but I still felt Him with us the entire time, watching us with His hands shadowing to catch us if we fell.

I like to think of it in this way: When a baby is learning to walk, the parent is always close by. They watch their child gain strength and balance to put one foot in front of the other as they learn to walk. There will be times when the baby falls and scrapes her knee or bumps his head, and it's going to hurt. The parent is always there to swoop them up, care for them, tell them it's going to be OK, put them back down, and say, "Keep going, you've got this." The parent knows that eventually the child will be surefooted and won't fall or bump her head—but the only way for the toddler to get through this is to just keep going.

It was during that time that I felt I became a man with God allowing me to walk on my own.

If you are walking through something similar, or going through a different kind of turbulent season in your life, this may be the last thing you want to hear or read. But I sincerely want to say, "Keep going, you've got this."

The outcome may or may not look as you had hoped in the beginning, but if you allow yourself to trust the Lord, He will take care of you.

A Letter from Tina Rowe

To be touched by supernatural hand of the Lord is a gift to be treasured forever! I was blessed to be a part of Rosemary's miracles. To see the faith she had during and after the loss of her children inspired me to strive for the same level of faith.

To stand by her side and be placed in the position to guide and protect her precious family for the birth of Mary Alice was such an honor. Seeing the love and joy she had those precious hours she and Bobby were able to spend with their daughter was, at times, overwhelming.

I was pushed into a new place of trusting in the Lord by having the blessing of being her midwife during the birth of her son. Prayer, tears, and joy were never more abundant than during that birth. God's grace abounded, and Rosemary was given the gift of a child after more loss than most could endure.

To then come full circle and be able to experience the Popes give birth to a daughter in the room I built to honor Mary Alice is, well . . . difficult to put into words.

Rosemary has so many gifts. I was honored to be her midwife. The Lord has shown His mercy and grace and has taught me how to be a midwife with full faith and trust in Him!

God bless this beloved family!

A Letter from Linda Turner

I love the Pope Family so very much! Bobby, Rosemary, Buddy, Lucy, and Casey have forever impacted my life. I will never ever forget Mary Alice or Buddy's births. Not to take away from how special Casey's was. I keep Mary Alice's pictures on my phone and look at them periodically and think of her, and then I am reminded how much joy I felt to help deliver Buddy after Mary Alice's time.

Forever etched in my memory is this story of overcoming. To be honest, these are the two most meaningful births I have experienced. I will always remember the hospital staff handing Mary Alice over for me to listen to her heartbeat, anoint her with oil, and pray over her. Being there with Bobby and Rosemary for the hours Mary Alice lived was such a privilege and an honor.

Being asked to be Rosemary's midwife with Casey's pregnancy meant so much to me. I treasure the trust Rosemary gave me and what her family means to me.

Rosemary is an amazing woman of God and carries so much strength. I look up to her. The grace she displayed during her losses and hardships and how she continued to praise God through it all is an inspiration.

Jesus knew I needed Rosemary in my life, and I am so grateful for knowing her.

Rosemary's Playlist

1. "Held" – Natalie Grant
This song hits me right in the feels every time. It overwhelms me in a great deal of emotion that ultimately ends in peace with the fact that through it all, I was held.

2. "You Never Let Go" – David Crowder Band
This song played on repeat for several months. Its nice, slow melody soothed my soul and brought me rest when my emotions would get the best of me.

3. "Worn" – Tenth Avenue North
Being tired from life, this song expresses the desire for things to get better. Hoping that everything that is making one weary isn't for nothing. It's like a one-last-cry-for-help.

4. "Even When It Hurts" – Hillsong
This is a recent song that always takes me back to the weekend I decided I was to carry Mary Alice for as long as I could despite the probable outcome. I was so hurt mentally, physically, and emotionally. Listening to this song, I can feel the pain of the artist, and I nod right along remembering just how weak the pain made me feel.

5. "By Your Side" – Tenth Avenue North
It was as if God was speaking to me: "Child, don't give up on

me." He did it through the lyrics of this song. My heart still warms and a smile appears on my face when I hear this song.

6. "It Is Well" – Bethel Music and Kristene DiMarco

This is a recent song and wasn't around when I went through those trials. If it was, you can believe this song would have been on repeat. Even when my eyes could not see, I knew who was ultimately in control. The only way for me to survive was to put my trust in Christ so that, through everything, I could remind myself to sit back and be well.

7. "Times" – Tenth Avenue North

In times of feeling unwanted, or ashamed for things you've done, said, or thought, God is still there. This song shares how God has always been there.

8. "Breath of Heaven" – Natalie Grant

Being pregnant during Christmastime and knowing I'd soon say goodbye to the child I carried brought me closer to the story of Jesus' birth and his mother, Mary. This song depicts my thoughts from this time perfectly; it's sung from Mary's point of view.

9. "Beautiful" – MercyMe

Although this is a song meant for self-worth and dedicated to the artists' living children, I felt the lyrics spoke of my unborn child, who was deemed "incompatible with life."

10. "What Faith Can Do" – Kutless

When I was ready to throw in the towel, this song gave me the courage to muster up a little more faith to keep going.

11. "History" – Bethel Music and Alton Eugene

A new song that I listen to with a smile. God and me have a history together that goes "way, way back." He's been with me through it all, which has brought us closer together.

12. "You Can Have Me" – Sidewalk Prophets

This is a song of surrender. When I walked the hard road to motherhood and realized things were out of my control, I gave myself to God. My thinking was: surely there is something good that can be made of these tragedies. The title of this book was inspired by this song; it was only fitting it be included on this list.

Resources

- **Now I Lay Me Down To Sleep (NILMDTS)**
Organization of volunteer photographers who will take wonderful professional pictures for families who are suffering the loss of a baby.
www.nowilaymedowntosleep.org

- **I Will Carry You**
Book written by Angie Smith. Angie shares her powerful story of losing her child, weaving it together with the biblical story of Lazarus. This is a book about the sacred dance of grief and joy.
www.angiesmithonline.com

- **Deeper Shade of Grace**
Book by Bernadette Keaggy. Bernadette writes with candor about the hurt and confusion that shook her to the core of her being. Through her own journey she leads us not to simple answers but to spiritual understanding. Bernadette's thoughtful, inspiring account offers profound insight to anyone who has ever looked at life's moments of happiness and loss and wondered why.
This is an older book that may require a little digging around the Internet to find, but it is well worth the search.

- **A Grief Observed**
Book by famed twentieth-century theologian C.S. Lewis.

Lewis's honest reflection on the fundamental issues of life, death, and faith in the midst of loss. This work contains his concise, genuine reflections of that period. This is a beautiful and unflinchingly honest record of how even a stalwart believer can lose all sense of meaning in the universe, and how he can gradually regain his bearings.

Can be found nearly anywhere books are sold.

• The Lord of Birth

Written by Jennifer Vanderlaan. A devotional Bible study for pregnancy that teaches and reminds women to put their hope and trust in our Lord. I was given this book at the beginning of my last pregnancy and instantly liked what it had to offer. As a seasoned mother who has experienced seven pregnancies, I wished I had found this devotional years ago.

www.birthingnaturally.net

• Mothers of the Bible

Written by Ann Spangler and Jean E. Syswerda. This devotional study takes you inside the lives of twelve biblical mothers whose struggles to live with faith and courage are much like yours. Through their successes and failures alike, these women from long ago will encourage you and strengthen you in your challenging and rewarding role as a mother.

Can be found nearly anywhere books are sold.

• James Avery Charms

Beautiful, well-crafted, quality charms for all occasions. These make stunning keepsakes of children that have passed. Engraving is available and can be worn on a bracelet or necklace.

www.jamesavery.com

- **Willow Tree Statues**

Small figure-like statues known for their simplicity, but detail, in the gestures in these statues. There are several statues to choose from for sympathy or remembrance that are perfect as a thoughtful gift.

www.willowtree.com

- **Scentsy Buddies**

Stuffed animals with a zipper in the back in which you can place a favorite scent. Ideal for a mother of empty arms needing something to hold.

- **BabyCenter Community**

A website dedicated to women in all walks of parenthood who can connect with others walking through similar stages of life: trying to conceive, infertility, pregnancy, pregnancy loss, baby milestones, and beyond.

community.babycenter.com

Endnotes

1. Laura Ingalls Wilder, *Little House in the Big Woods* (New York: HarperCollins Publishers, 1960), p. 2.

2. C.S. Lewis, *A Grief Observed* (New York, HarperCollins Publishers, 1994), p. 26.

3. Ann Spangler and Jean E. Syswerda, *Mothers of the Bible: A Devotional* (Grand Rapids, MI: Zondervan, 2006), pp. 16, 17.

4. Ibid., p. 115.

5. American Pregnancy Association, http://americanpregnancy.org/getting-pregnant/understanding-ovulation/. Last updated October 26, 2018. © 2018.

6. Lewis, *A Grief Observed*, p. 56.

7. Randi Fannon, Facebook comment, https://www.facebook.com/rosemary.a.pope/posts/10156681986449453, posted March 6, 2018. © 2018.

8. Lewis, p. 3.

9. Lewis, p. 33.

10. Angie Smith, *I Will Carry You: The Sacred Dance of Grief and Joy* (Nashville, TN: B&H Publishing Group, 2010), p. 32.

11. Passion Growers, http://www.passiongrowers.com/web/ot/colors.asp. © 2011.

12. Spangler and Syswerda, p. 144.

13. Beth Moore, *A Heart Like His: Intimate Reflections on the Life of David* (Nashville, TN: B&H Publishing Group, 2012), p. 190.

14. Lewis, p. 52.

15. Jon Micah Sumerall, YouTube video, "Kutless–What Faith Can Do–Song Explanation," https://www.youtube.com/watch?v=HXQNQmed6PY. Posted February 2, 2010. © 2010.

16. Kristine Tawater, Facebook post, https://www.facebook.com/lovemy5/posts/10215528275497621, posted April 4, 2018. © 2018 Kristine Tawater.

17. Tawater, Facebook post as cited above. © 2018 Kristine Tawater.